THE PRIMER FOR
INSTITUTIONAL RESEARCH

Edited by
William E. Knight

THE ASSOCIATION FOR INSTITUTIONAL RESEARCH
Number Fourteen
Resources in Institutional Research

©2003 Association for Institutional Research
222 Stone Building
Florida State University
Tallahassee, FL 32306-4462

ISBN 1-882393-10-4

Contents

Introduction

William E. Knight
Bowling Green State University

Despite the maturation of the profession, the question, *What is institutional research?*, seems to be perpetual. While many of us have attempted to provide answers to family, friends and colleagues, the responses we often get suggest that our answers are somewhat lacking: "Just as long as you're happy, dear, and the work is steady." "I've worked here for 25 years and had no idea anyone did this kind of work." and "I can't believe they really pay you for doing that!" Some of the more meaningful definitions have included: "research conducted within an institution of higher education in order to provide information which supports planning, policy formation, and decision making" (Saupe, 1981, p. 1); an activity having " . . . to do with what decision makers need to know about an institution, its educational objectives, goals and purposes, environmental factors, processes, and structures to more widely use its resources, more successfully attain its objectives and goals, and to demonstrate integrity and accountability in so doing" (Dressell, 1981, p. 237); and "a critical intermediary function that links the educational, managerial, and information functions of higher education institutions and functions" (Peterson, 1985, p. 5). Terenzini (1993) built upon the idea of institutional research as a form of "organizational intelligence" that requires three types of personal competence and institutional understanding for successful practice. He suggested ways in which each of the three types of knowledge and skills can be gained.

Given diversity in both the levels of professional knowledge and skills held by institutional researchers and, the ways in which they have been acquired (Knight, Moore, and Coperthwaite, 1997), it is incumbent upon the leaders of the profession to provide a variety of professional development opportunities to both new and experienced practitioners. *A Primer on Institutional Research* (1987), *The Primer for Institutional Research* (1992), and *Strategies for the Practice of Institutional Research: Concepts, Resources, and Applications* (1994) are three publications from the Association for Institutional Research (AIR) designed to provide an introduction to some of the more common institutional research issues, methods, and resources for newcomers and to provide a means for veterans to update their capabilities. Those volumes, and this update, serve as just some of the many professional development resources available to institutional researchers; several other resources will be highlighted in the concluding chapter.

The purpose of this volume is to update and expand upon these previous works. I was very fortunate to be able to assemble a group of highly talented authors, whose efforts represent a significant contribution to the profession. John Muffo opens the book with a chapter on institutional research support for college and university accountability, including focus upon institutional accreditation; disciplinary accreditation; new program approval; internal program review; data reporting to federal, state, commercial, and inter-institutional agencies; special studies; and state-mandated assessment activities and performance studies. Institutional research support for assessment is always an important topic. Karen Bauer discusses definitions, principles, and purposes of assessment as well as levels and key steps in assessment projects; she ends by showcasing examples of assessment measures for researchers.

Michael Middaugh and Heather Kelly Isaacs focus on faculty activity and productivity. Their chapter highlights the conditions in American higher education that mandate the development of instructional productivity and cost measures on campus, provides a discussion of framing the appropriate language for describing faculty duties and responsibilities, and focuses on the need for providing practical management information for decision support. Rich Howard and Gerald McLaughlin highlight the analytical and political issues involved in faculty salary analysis. Their work includes important background issues for consideration, a conceptual model for faculty salary analysis, recent developments in faculty salary analysis and points to consider, and a series of steps that institutional researchers should use when asked to carry out faculty salary analyses.

In their discussion of enrollment management, Rick Kroc and Gary Hanson provide an overview of student recruitment, including the educational pipeline, enrollment projections, and financial aid; student flow, including academic preparation, the curriculum, academic and student support programs, graduation and retention rates, and issues beyond graduation, and support for enrollment management; including organizational structures, necessary IR technical and analytical skills, data sources, and communicating results of enrollment management studies. They conclude with a consideration of the future of enrollment management. In their chapter on peer institutions, Deb Teeter and Paul Brinkman highlight selecting peer institutions and conducting inter-institutional data exchanges; they focus on both the political and technical issues of choosing peers, as well as issues involved with acquiring and working with peer data.

Tod Massa's chapter on using the Web for institutional research represents an important addition to this *Primer* that will be beneficial to veterans, as well as new, institutional research practitioners. Tod focuses upon the Web as an organic medium, connective sense-making, applying the Web to the IR life-cycle, and concludes with a look to the future. John Milam's chapter on using national datasets for postsecondary education research is a valuable resource for today's institutional researchers; his work focuses on using different lenses for finding data, understanding major data collections, getting access to datasets, and emerging trends in data collection. Andrew Luna and Tara Pearson inform institutional researchers about the importance of records management and describe how to create an effective records management program within an IR office. Finally, I provide a concluding chapter on additional professional development opportunities for institutional researchers.

The efforts of many additional persons who have contributed to the development of this volume must be acknowledged. These contributors include Richard Howard, Editor of the AIR *Resources in Institutional Research* series; the AIR Publications Committee and AIR Board; Terry Russell, AIR Executive Director and other AIR central office staff; the copy editor; and, last but surely not least, Christine Call, AIR Assistant Director for Marketing and Communications, whose professionalism and dedication allows the publication process to proceed so smoothly. Any errors that remain, of course, are solely my responsibility.

References

Dressel, P. L. (1981). *The shaping of institutional research and planning.* Research in Higher Education, 14. (pp. 229-258).

Knight, W. E., Moore, M. E., and Coperthwaite, C. A. (1997). *Institutional research: Knowledge, skills, and perceptions of effectiveness.* Research in Higher Education, 38. (pp. 419-433).

Middaugh, M. F., Trusheim, D. W. and Bauer, K. W. (Eds.) (1994). Strategies for the practice of institutional research: Concepts, resources, and applications. Tallahassee, FL: The Association for Institutional Research.

Muffo, J. A. and McLaughlin, G. W. (Eds.) (1987). A primer on institutional research. Tallahassee, FL: The Association for Institutional Research.

Peterson, M. W. (1985). *Institutional research: An evolutionary perspective.* In M. Corcoran and M. W. Peterson (Eds.). New Directions for Institutional Research: No. 46. Institutional Research in Transition. San Francisco, CA: Jossey-Bass. (pp. 5-15).

Saupe, J. L. (1981). The functions of institutional research. Tallahassee, FL: The Association for Institutional Research.

Terenzini, P. T. (1993). *On the nature of institutional research and the knowledge and skills it requires.* Research in Higher Education, 34. (pp. 1-10).

Whitley, M. A., Porter, J. D. and Fenske, R. H. (Eds.) (1992). The primer for institutional research. Tallahassee, FL: The Association for Institutional Research.

Chapter 1
Institutional Research Support of Accountability

John A. Muffo
Virginia Tech

Introduction

Accountability is a popular term in higher education these days. It refers to colleges and universities being held responsible for using their resources in an efficient and effective manner in order to produce the best education possible at the most reasonable cost. In many regards it is a reaction to the traditional condition, cited by a former board member many years ago, who said that the institutions of postsecondary education in his state could not explain what they did with the money they were given during the prior year. All they knew was they needed more of it the following year. Such perceived responses are very difficult to understand for the business and professional people who constitute the higher education boards of trustees, both public and private, as well as state-level boards. They tend to be accustomed to "bottom line" or profit-making environments and have difficulty understanding the lack of accountability measures in colleges and universities. The tendency, therefore, is to require that some be developed.

The kind of accountability discussed in this chapter is not normally financial accountability, though that is sometimes touched upon in certain reporting activities. The type of accountability referenced here is less legalistic and financial, as accountants might be concerned with, and is, instead, more performance oriented. In institutional research, the focus tends to be more on performance auditing than on financial auditing. The former asks how well the money was spent, while the latter addresses whether or not it was spent properly, i.e., within legal and other acceptable financial bounds. Only occasionally is a college or university accused of financial improprieties. Unfortunately, accusations of mismanagement and instructional malfeasance are much more common.

One approach that has been employed is merging financial data with performance data to create efficiency measures of various sorts. There is a long history of developing measures such as costs per student credit hour, square footage of buildings per student credit hour, faculty and staff members per headcount and full-time equivalent student, etc. While most often associated with budgeting, such data also have been used to identify the relative efficiency of institutions, especially public ones. The use of such measures has driven accountability in the sense that they have been employed to restrict institutional resource ambitions.

There are a number of ways of evaluating accountability internally and externally. One common method is comparison: *How are we doing compared to our closest competition or to our "peers" ?* Another method is trend analysis:

How has the number of applicants to a program, for example, changed over time? Yet another approach uses targets: *Have we reduced our costs by five percent as planned? Is this program as successful as the benchmark one at another institution?*

It is logical to question why so much attention has been focused on the performance aspects of accountability in recent years. Several answers to that question have been suggested, and probably all of the proposed answers have had some influence. One suggestion relates to the large percentage of students now going to college. When more than half of all high school graduates are attending college, there is less mystique regarding it. "Familiarity breeds contempt" might apply here. In addition, many families are impacted by higher education, financially and otherwise. More complaints, whether valid or not, are passed along to lawmakers and other influential people, themselves undergraduate alumni, at cocktail parties and over back fences. Communication of concerns is easier as well. Traditional telephones, cell phones, faxes, e-mails, the Internet, magazines, newspapers, and improved transportation all contribute to a world full of supposed experts expressing their opinions on higher education. The call for accountability happened first at the K-12 level; now it is happening at the postsecondary level.

Another related factor has to do with the sheer amount of resources now devoted to higher education. The June 30, 2000, value of the Harvard endowment alone was reported to be nearly $19 billion, while the public University of Texas system had more than $10 billion. Single private gifts of $100 – $200+ million are no longer shocking. Capital campaigns of more than $1 billion are nearly commonplace. These contributions are in addition to the multi-billions that the state and federal governments provide annually. In short, higher education is now a major industry in North America and elsewhere. Once an industry or individual institutions reach these sizes, people naturally want to know how all of that money is being spent, especially as more and more is being requested. As an old saying goes, "If you take dad's money, you have to take his guff." In this case dad is the public, higher education is taking the money, and accountability is one of the consequences of that.

Most discussions of accountability refer to external aspects. However, for many institutions of higher education, public as well as private, internal accountability is most important. Internal accountability deals with balancing the budget. A lack of students results in less funding, leading to painful reduction decisions or perhaps even closing. Accountability in this sense has to do with attracting, retaining, and graduating good students. These types of data gathering activities may begin long before the students enter and conclude many years after they have graduated.

In addition to increased external and internal scrutiny, other possible explanations for the rise of accountability include the ability to easily gather, analyze, and report data using computers, as well as the general trend in our society to question everything. The reality is that all of these factors probably have contributed to an increased interest in accountability. The remainder of the chapter will discuss different ways in which institutional researchers support accountability activities.

Accreditation

Institutional accreditation by regional (in the United States) or national (in most other countries) bodies is one of the most important, and sometimes the most challenging, ways in which institutional researchers become involved in accountability matters. A great deal of organization, data gathering, and reporting go into regional accrediting reports every five to 10 years, depending on the region and the institution. Even shorter periods are permitted in between updates. They often are conducted on an annual or biennial basis, depending on how well the institution performed during the prior visit. Regional accrediting agencies tend to want to review the numbers that institutional researchers compile and report: enrollments, enrollment trends, student and faculty qualifications, faculty workloads, grade distributions, space allocation, special studies conducted, etc. Additional questions raised during the site visits may generate even more requests for data, sometimes while the visiting team is still on campus. Writing the reports and dealing with the site visits frequently takes a good deal of institutional researchers' time during the period prior to and during the visit.

Why is regional accreditation so important? Why do colleges and universities spend so much time, energy, and money on these processes? Aside from institutional improvement, the purpose usually stated in public pronouncements, two major activities depend on accreditation: acceptance of transfer credit by other institutions and student eligibility for federal financial aid, including guaranteed loans. A few colleges and universities, prestigious ones in particular, may not be very concerned about the former, but virtually all institutions take the latter seriously. Without federal student financial aid, most campuses would be forced to reduce their budgets significantly because of declining enrollment, and a number would have to cease operating altogether.

The more informal, but no less serious, reason that accreditation is important has to do with institutional pride and perceived quality. A poor accreditation report implies major operational problems and poor leadership. More than one president and numerous other administrators have found themselves seeking other employment after negative accreditation reviews. So, if college and university personnel seem nervous about putting the report together and preparing for the visit, they have a right to be. Their jobs, not to mention institutional and presidential prestige, could depend on a positive report from the visiting team.

The other type of accreditation is disciplinary accreditation, where an academic program is approved. These processes are much more focused than regional accreditation is, and the institutional research office may have little or no involvement. Sometimes the academic unit seeking accreditation will request support for compiling some of the required data. The amount of data requested,

3

as well as the data definitions, may vary substantially, so these efforts can be strenuous also, depending on the academic unit being considered for accreditation. In recent years the disciplinary accrediting bodies have become more outcomes oriented, encouraged by the federal and state governments. As a result, the burden has become to prove achievement in student learning in addition to more traditional input variables such as faculty qualifications, classroom and laboratory space, equipment, etc.

Why is disciplinary accreditation so important? In some cases employers do not know which programs are accredited by specific organizations; accreditation is simply inconsequential. In other cases it may be necessary to graduate from an accredited program in order to be eligible to be licensed in a specific field. Graduate schools sometimes favor alumni of accredited programs as well. In most instances, however, it comes down to faculty pride in the discipline. Accredited programs are recognized as being high quality ones by others in the field; it is worth the time, effort, and money involved for the local program to obtain such recognition. In addition, to the chagrin of many senior administrators, accreditation frequently is used as a lever to lobby for more human and financial resources for the program. This is one of the primary reasons for senior administrator announcements about the need to get disciplinary accreditation under control and reduce the number of units seeking disciplinary accreditation.

Program Approval

Most states have a program approval process for all new academic programs, often at private as well as public institutions. Certainly the publics must show that there is a need for a program and that it does not unnecessarily duplicate other programs. Usually the private institutions have a similar, albeit usually less intrusive, process as well. With off-campus distance learning, and multi-campus/multi-state systems like the University of Phoenix, states find themselves quite busy just monitoring and approving programs.

Often the institutional research role in program approval can be one more akin to market research than to more traditional activities. For example, one might be asked to study census data, manpower projections, other workforce data, and/or to survey employer needs after summarizing existing programs at sister institutions. Program approval frequently requires student assessment data, often with a follow-up on the program several years after initial approval, to ensure that program objectives for student learning are being met as promised.

External Reporting

Although not necessarily directly related to accountability, probably the first and most common connection of institutional research professionals to it is through external reporting to federal and state agencies, private entities, and voluntary data sharing groups. The Damocles sword of student financial aid hangs over some of the federal reports that must be filed. Failure to report crime statistics, for example, can lead to a loss of eligibility for student financial aid. Many of the other reports, such as the Integrated Postsecondary Education Data System (IPEDS) series, are supposedly voluntary; however, most institutions cooperate out of fear of federal government retribution. Once the data become readily available, now on easy-to-use compact disks or CDs, institutions can be and are compared to each other on various data elements. Accountability arises when the comparisons are used to set policy, usually at the state level.

In addition to federal reporting, the states typically gather a series of reports from the colleges and universities. Often the private institutions can choose whether or not to participate; however, the publics usually are not given an option. Private institutions may be more inclined to comply if state student financial aid hangs in the balance. The state-level data on such measures as graduation rates, admissions standards, student transfer rates, success of remedial students, etc. are used to set state policy. Increasingly these data are utilized in place of funding formulas to determine, at least in part, institutional allocations. Mirroring other areas of accountability, in recent years the focus has shifted from inputs to outcomes.

Private publications such as *U.S. News & World Report* and *Peterson's Guides* in the United States, *McLean's* in Canada, and *LeMonde* in France gather data from colleges and universities for supposedly informational purposes. Best known among these are the *U.S. News & World Report* rankings. Though theoretically voluntary, those institutions refusing to submit data will not be mentioned positively. Public statements to the contrary, most presidents like to see their institutions included among the top 10 or top 25 and share that information liberally. Those not ranked as highly discuss the methodological weaknesses of the rankings when questioned in public. Whether one agrees with such rankings or not, they constitute a very public form of accountability. The original data for these rankings most often are reported by institutional research offices.

The one truly voluntary type of reporting sometimes used for accountability purposes derives from voluntary data exchanges. There are a number of such exchanges in which institutions voluntarily agree to share information with other, similar ones. Typically the data are not identified by the name of the college or university. The data can be useful for management purposes. For instance, they may indicate that similar institutions with like numbers of students have fewer or more faculty, larger or smaller student service operations, etc. Usually this information is employed for internal decision-making; nevertheless, the resulting actions can be quite substantial in some cases, proving that accountability is not always externally driven.

Internal Program Review

Internal program review takes place when a program or unit undergoes a thorough study of its operations. While this sometimes occurs as a singular event or *ad hoc* study, normally program reviews occur on some kind of regularized schedule. These reviews tend to be more comprehensive than annual reports or other, more limited reviews, such as an assessment report. A thorough program review might well be an exhaustive study from top to bottom. This may include data regarding faculty, students, and staff. Teaching, research, and service roles may be examined in units with all or some of these responsibilities. A program review often involves external experts serving as reviewers or consultants. These can be even more thorough than disciplinary accreditation visits, depending on the criteria used in the accreditation processes and those of the program reviews. The latter might take a closer look at financing, for example, or planning or leadership than the former would, though many of these factors tend to overlap.

A program review is a natural place for an institutional researcher. Who better to provide many of the various objective data snapshots needed to determine what the unit has been doing and how well it has been doing it? Because the institutional researcher is not a part of the unit being reviewed, the data have more credibility, since the provider will not benefit from adjusting the numbers in any way. In addition, the institutional research office can provide comparative data from similar units and perhaps from those at peer institutions. These can assist the reviewers, internal and external, allowing them to focus their attention on specific factors. For instance, reviewers may be interested in knowing: that a certain unit seems to be serving twice as many students per faculty member as similar units; or that the faculty research rate by various measures is higher or lower than expected; or that there does not appear to be much evidence of service; or that there seems to be a lot more productivity than peer units report being able to accomplish.

Portions of the data will reside in existing institutional databases, often reported in some form already; however, sometimes new analyses and data gathering will be required. Many of the most important and interesting questions are not easily answered by standard reports; that's where creative institutional research can make a real difference. Obviously, good communication with both the reviewers and the unit being reviewed is critical, as is the confidence of all in the data produced. In the end, if the veracity of the data were not important for program review, anybody could produce the numbers, leaving one less role to be played by the institutional researcher.

Special Studies

Special studies are similar to program reviews, taking a thorough look at a unit, program, or policy. They are different, however, in that they can be much more focused, examining for example only one aspect of a situation. Because of their focused nature, special studies tend to be conducted on a more occasional basis, when questions arise, rather than on a regular schedule. They often also require a great deal of creativity to arrive at even tentative conclusions.

Examples of special studies are numerous. The following are some recent ones at just one university:

- *The 1.6 grade point average* – For many, many years, a freshman student needed only a 1.6 GPA to progress to the sophomore year,

6

with the levels gradually moving up to 2.0 in the senior year. A brief institutional research study, requested by no one external to the office, showed that fewer than five percent of students with a 1.6 at the end of the first year ever graduated. This was shared casually with a senior faculty member. The policy has now been changed, and more first-year students are achieving better than in the past. This is especially true of those who put forth the minimum amount of effort to stay enrolled.

- *The Mathematics Emporium* – Several million dollars has been invested in a Mathematics Emporium. This investment is the result of several institutional research and assessment studies pointing to the need for improved retention in freshman mathematics courses and the effectiveness of hands-on work in assisting student learning. Computer assisted instruction via the Emporium was the primary method selected to address the matter, but faculty in other departments questioned so much money being spent in one place with no externally verified evidence of whether it was making a difference or not. The institutional research and assessment offices were asked to do a thorough study addressing, specifically, the issue of improved student learning. The outsiders (to the Department of Mathematics) were able to estimate how many more students were retained and at what cost. The Mathematics Emporium remains a vibrant unit, even serving some students not currently enrolled in mathematics courses.

- *Other special studies* – These have included studies determining: the university's core values; the viability of the university's European Center; the desirability of a campus/town bus system; problems in transitioning from a quarter to a semester system; the effectiveness of the honor code; the effectiveness of campus alcohol policies; the desirability of increasing the required TOEFL (Teaching of English as a Foreign Language) scores for graduate students; and many other topics.

One could derive a long list of special studies of units, programs, policies, and projects on most campuses with long-existing institutional research functions. They can be very useful tools for the management of the organization. At the same time, they can be among the most challenging, but interesting, tasks undertaken by institutional research professionals.

A type of special study that deserves mention here is one that determines the effectiveness of a project, in particular one that is externally funded. Many United States government agencies, such as the National Science Foundation (NSF) and the Department of Agriculture (USDA), require evaluations, preferably external ones, of projects aimed at the improvement of instruction and consequent student learning. More and more institutional research and assessment professionals are being asked to assist with evaluating such projects for their effectiveness. Because the evaluators are external to the unit being evaluated, having a strong evaluation component can present an opportunity to strengthen funding proposals. The evaluations often are time-consuming but can also be interesting. They can be helpful to the institution and units involved, while potentially generating external funds for the institutional research and assessment offices in the process. (Don't do it for free, or you won't have time to do anything else!)

For State-Supported Institutions

In addition to the types of statistical reporting mentioned earlier relating to state-supported institutions, in recent years another kind has increased in popularity among state governments: assessment reporting and its progeny, performance indicators reporting. Assessment reporting basically asks institutions to develop methods of measuring student learning, usually externally verifiable methods, then bases a portion of the funding allocated for each institution upon the degree of success in improving the student learning as planned. Often colleges and universities are measured against historical standards and are expected to improve on past performance in order to acquire all of the "incentive" funding. Although Tennessee is perhaps the best known state for such assessment systems, many others employ similar complete or partial approaches as well.

A frustrating aspect of assessment systems for state policy makers has been the difficulty in comparing the performance of different institutions using them. Despite some public pronouncements to the contrary, it seems that many in state government wish to compare institutions and rank them like teams in sports leagues. As a result of this desire and the general lack of numbers resulting from the assessment approach, a large number of states are now utilizing performance indicators. These are numbers that can be tied to policy issues, encouraging institutions to manage themselves in more desirable (from the state's point of view) ways. Performance indicators frequently are tied to funding. Though most states keep this portion to five or 10 percent, they supposedly are tied to the majority of funding that colleges and universities receive in South Carolina. Examples of indicators include a host of measures: first to second year retention rates; five or six year graduation rates; percentage of student credit hours taught by tenure-track faculty; minority student recruitment and retention rates; space utilization ratios; accounting standards being met; etc. Institutional researchers have spent many hours gathering and refining such indicators in recent years.

Conclusion

As can be seen above, institutional researchers play a central role in accountability efforts; they often have the primary responsibility for various aspects of accountability. The key to staying abreast of the constantly changing accountability scene is participation in continuing education activities through state, regional, and national institutional research organizations. Accountability is a world that changes quickly and often. One needs the assistance of others in order to keep from being left behind.

Chapter 2
Assessment for Institutional Research:
Guidelines and Resources

Karen W. Bauer
University of Delaware

Introduction

Although assessment has existed in various forms since the beginning of higher education, we have witnessed an increase in public scrutiny and calls for strengthened accreditation efforts within the past 30 years. Because of this heightened emphasis on assessment, institutional researchers must apportion some of their time to assessment tasks. As experts in data collection, storage, and analysis, institutional research (IR) professionals are often looked upon to design, implement, and report on various assessment activities. Thus, along with the myriad of daily tasks you will complete in IR, you will likely become involved in your institution's assessment plan and/or implementation.

What is Assessment?

Although the topic is frequently discussed, many higher education officials hold different interpretations of assessment. Definitions and discussions about assessment abound; the references listed at the end of this chapter provide more detailed discussions, however, we will briefly discuss a few definitions and approaches. Dary Erwin defines assessment as "the systematic basis for making inferences about the learning and development of students...the process of defining, selecting, designing, collecting, analyzing, interpreting, and using information to increase students' learning and development" (Erwin, 1991, pp. 14-19). Ernest Boyer and Peter Ewell (1988) approach assessment broadly, noting that it provides information about students, curricula or programs, institutions, or about entire systems of institutions. Fred Volkwein, an IR colleague and leader in the field, maintains that "assessment is a process, not a product; it is a beginning, not an end" (Bauer & Volkwein, 2000). Professor Thomas Angelo (1995, in AAHE, 2002) cogently sums up assessment as:

> "...a means for focusing our collective attention... examining assumptions and creating a shared academic culture dedicated to continuously improving the quality of higher education learning. Assessment requires making expectations and standards for quality explicit and public... Systematically gathering evidence on how well performance matches those expectations and standards... Analyzing and interpreting the evidence, and using the resulting information to document, explain, and improve performance...."(p.7)

Assessment, then, is not simply a one-time survey on student mastery of a concept, nor a simple series of inventories. Certainly, mastery of knowledge can, and should, be part of an assessment plan, but it is only one facet of a comprehensive plan. A good assessment plan requires dedicated effort to ensure the articulation of measurable goals and objectives, systematically gathering evidence of performance (multiple measures during a specified period of time), interpreting the findings in the context of the specific campus and student body, and incorporating those results in curricular and programmatic changes that will again be assessed in a cyclical fashion.

Ideally, assessment techniques should not be an intrusion in the classroom, infringe on academic freedom, nor be incorporated in your faculty and staff evaluation system. Keeping evaluation for promotion and tenure separate enables the researcher to use assessment as part of the existing plans to gauge the strength of the institution, in turn, promoting self-examination, critical questioning, and opportunities for renewal. Realizing that assessment should not be viewed as an easy, one-time task, the ongoing, cyclical nature of assessment necessarily means that it is conceptually, politically, and administratively a complicated, but highly challenging process!

The terms assessment and evaluation are often used interchangeably. Some higher education officials think of these terms synonymously, while others believe there is a difference between the two terms. I prefer to think of evaluation as a subset of assessment. With a prescribed research question and specific method, we might choose to evaluate a student's progress in mastering math concepts or document students' evaluation of food services. These separate evaluations, however, are subsets of an institution's larger assessment of students' learning and campus services. Because this discussion focuses on the larger, comprehensive process, this chapter primarily refers to assessment.

There are many good references available to assist in understanding the nuances of assessment, aspects that are appropriate for a specific campus explains how the IR office can contribute to your institution's overall assessment plan. In addition to specific books, such as Gray and Banta's (1997) discussion of campus level assessment, worthwhile information is available on the AIR Web site (http://www.airweb.org and click on IR Resources) and through case studies from a variety of institutions (Banta, Lund, Black, & Oberlander, 1996). In addition, the American Association for Higher Education (AAHE) has several Web- and print-based resources that can assist in understanding assessment. From AAHE's home page (http://www.aahe.org) researchers will find informative online readings about assessment (http://www.aahe.org/assessment/assess_links.htm#readings), assessment policies (http://www.aahe.org/bulletin/may2.htm#policies), electronic discussion lists (http://www.aahe.org/assessment/assess_links.htm#listservs), and specific articles such as *Fair Assessment Practices* (Suskie, 2000) and two sets of *Principles of Good Practice* (AAHE, 1992). Following the *Seven Principles of Good Practice in Undergraduate Education* (Chickering & Gamson, 1987), a task force of knowledgeable educators (including Pat Cross, Peter Ewell, Trudy Banta and Elaine El-Khawas) collaborated to delineate the *AAHE Nine Principles of Good Practice in Assessing*

Student Learning (AAHE, 1992). These principles consolidate ideas about effective assessment practice and can provide a guide for future assessment plans and implementation. The nine principles are as follows:

1. Assessment of student learning begins with educational values.

2. Assessment is most effective when it reflects an understanding of learning as multidimensional, integrated, and revealed in performance over time.

3. Assessment works best when the programs it seeks to improve have clear, explicitly stated purposes.

4. Assessment requires attention to outcomes but also, and equally, to the experiences that lead to those outcomes.

5. Assessment works best when it is ongoing, not episodic.

6. Assessment fosters wider improvement when representatives across the educational community are involved.

7. Assessment makes a difference when it begins with issues of use and illuminates questions that people really care about.

8. Assessment is most likely to lead to improvement when it is part of a larger set of conditions that promote change.

9. Through assessment, educators meet responsibilities to students and to the public.

These nine principles offer an important framework that can be helpful in developing an overall assessment plan. Within such a framework, and for clarity to campus administrators, it may be helpful to also define a range of assessment modes. Thus, the researcher may find Harris and Bell's eight bipolar modes of assessment helpful (Harris & Bell, 1986):

- *Informal vs. formal*: ongoing observations and judgments versus planned and structured activities that have a particular purpose.

- *Formative vs. summative*: using the process of gathering evidence to facilitate improvement versus evidence collected for an external reason such as program continuance.

- *Process vs. product*: closely related but process examines the behaviors and structures occurring throughout the learning activity, while product is the measurable outcome.

- *Criterion-referenced vs. norm-referenced*: assessment activity intended to gauge improvement against a predetermined standard versus those intended to be used for comparison with peers.

- *Individual focused vs. group-focused*: assessment intended to help an individual student (or other individual) versus assessment directed at the group to address group trends, scores, or overall standards.

- *Continuous vs. end-point*: assessment performed periodically throughout the learning process versus that at the final or 'end' point in one's education.

- *Learner-judged vs. teacher-judged:* primarily useful in student assessment, the responsibility of assessment rests with the individual learner versus the instructor. Self, peer, and collaborative assessment play an important role in shifting the emphasis from teaching to learning.

- *Internal vs. external:* the individual has some control over the assessment plans and methods versus an external person or process established that controls the plans and methods for undertaking the assessment task.

Why is Assessment Necessary?

Assessment in higher education serves several important internal and external needs. It is important that an institution plans, and then monitors, activities that fulfill its mission. For higher education institutions, this requires the development and evaluation of programs and services that offer students a learning environment that maximizes their opportunities to learn. As the raison d'etre, assessment can help us revise curricula and improve the academic program. Via student portfolio or pre-post testing, it can document students' increases in writing or thinking skills. Assessment can also help strengthen student services and satisfaction, thereby improving student retention and enrollment management. For example, assessment can help monitor student satisfaction and use of health and wellness centers, career guidance, and residential living. If these programs are not supporting the needs of students, satisfaction and retention rates may be influenced.

In addition, continuous assessment enables an institution to focus on faculty and staff development. Often in the form of program review or institution-wide self-study, assessment can encourage faculty and staff initiative and collaboration. Furthermore, it can establish comparative markers for strategic planning, thus assisting in administrative policy development. When assessment becomes an integral part of the organization, it can have many positive and long-lasting benefits. For example, strong, measurable goals and objectives enable the institution to realize its mission, thus increasing its market advantage with peer institutions. This can, in turn, enrich development and external funding initiatives, and enable officials to demonstrate success in attaining the institution's mission and goals, thereby demonstrating institutional effectiveness.

Developing an assessment plan can also allow the researcher to carry out daily tasks more efficiently. It is recommended that a researcher work with senior leaders on campus to create a three- or five-year plan of IR assessment activities. If the IR office is the primary assessment office, the researcher will have a comprehensive, centralized picture of all campus assessment activities. If the institution is decentralized and assessment activities are performed through several offices and/or within each academic department, the researcher may want to share the list of IR assessment activities with others so that colleagues are informed. The sharing of assessment activities will help avoid duplicated efforts.

A second, growing reason for involvement in assessment relates to discipline and regional accreditation requirements. As John Muffo pointed out in the first chapter of this volume, most higher education institutions are required to perform some ongoing assessment for external accreditation requirements. United States colleges and universities seek accreditation from one of six regional agencies. In addition, many colleges and universities also seek discipline-specific accreditation that requires collection, analysis, and use of assessment information. Most likely the IR office will be called upon for various data needed to fulfill discipline-specific accreditation.

External accreditation generally encourages college and university officials to articulate a set of goals and objectives (set forth in the institution's mission) and provide evidence of how these goals are being met. Although not specifically a required task for accreditation, many institutions also include benchmarking, or peer comparison, as a way to gauge current status and/or progress. Although comparison with peers (either within a college or across similar colleges) usually does not offer trend information, it does require the appropriate normative reference group(s) be identified. Selecting a reference group offers the added benefit of a focused discussion on the characteristics that best define the institution's current status and/or future aspirations.

Levels of Assessment

Before beginning any assessment task, a researcher should understand the reason for completing the project and the consequent level(s) of assessment in higher education. As shown in Figure 1, assessment data can be collected for many reasons, and from a variety of different levels. An individual faculty member may wish to assess individual student progress in the classroom; the chairperson may wish to conduct a department-wide review; the provost or chancellor may coordinate institutional efforts to participate in a statewide assessment for all branch campuses. The methods and data collected may be similar or quite different, and in most instances, an assessment plan requires multiple data collection points. Assessment of student learning, for example, is like a puzzle. Each evaluation of learning is a piece of the puzzle that collectively provides a full picture of the student's learning process.

Figure 1. The Levels of Assessment in Higher Education

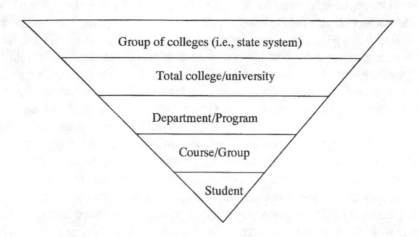

Strategies for Beginning an Assessment Project

Taking time to fully understand the problem at hand, as well as thinking through all phases, are important to the success of an assessment task. Often, many tasks must be juggled at once, and it is tempting to quickly rush through planning stages. However, thoughtful planning will increase the chances of success for the project. According to Upcraft & Schuh (1995) there are several important questions to ask when beginning an assessment task:

- Why is this assessment being conducted?
- Who/what will be assessed?
- How will they/it be assessed?
- Who will do the assessment?
- How will the results be analyzed?
- How will the results be communicated and to whom?
- How will the results be used?

When first beginning the project, a researcher may not have answers to all of the above questions. For example, as shown in Table 1, there are a variety of ways to assess student progress in the major. It is likely that a researcher will not tackle all of these methods of assessing student progress at once, thus advice may need to be sought from other colleagues, both on campus as well as within the IR profession. This will help the researcher clearly plan the assessment process. There may also be some indirect benefit to having other colleagues become invested in the project and/or offering their nod of approval, when beginning a project a researcher should consider his or her campus environment.

Table 1
Assessing Student Progress in the Major

- Portfolio Collection of Writings, other performance measures from matriculation to graduation (with expert of peer assessment)

- Research Project

- Capstone Course with Course-Embedded Assessment

- Comprehensive Exam or Proficiency Test

- Senior Thesis, Essay, or Other Writing Project

- Student/Faculty Retreat for Collective Assessment

- Internship or Field Work

- Analysis of Historical, Archival, or Transcript Data

- Alumni and/or Employee Surveys and Interviews

Key Steps in Assessment

There are five important steps to most assessment projects:
1. Specify the purposes, goals, and audiences;
2. Design methods and measures;
3. Carry out the data collection and analysis;
4. Communicate the findings to the audience; and,
5. Obtain feedback, follow-up, redesign, and improve.

1. Specify purposes, goals, and audiences. As a researcher begins, a new assessment project, it is important to identify the reason for undertaking the assessment, as well as the audience(s) for whom this information is important. Knowing, for example, that the assessment is requested from a new faculty member to be used as formative assessment for his/her improvement likely encourages the use of different methods and measures than if an assessment of the institution's general education curriculum was being performed. It is also crucial for the researcher to identify stakeholders in the assessment plan. One of the most frequent comments heard is the challenge to get campus members (i.e., faculty) involved and invested. To ensure success as well as to distribute the workload, the researcher may want to form a committee of campus faculty

and staff (and perhaps students too, depending on the project). Collaborative efforts offer the benefits of group brainstorming, a larger set of possible strategies, and psychological investment in the project.

2. Design the methods and measures. Once the researcher has a firm understanding for the purpose, goals, and audience, the next step is determining the methods and measures. Will data be gathered from a readily-available source, such as the institution's database or data warehouse, or must new data be collected? The variety of sources for campus assessment information should be examined: campus information systems; cohort tracking studies; department/ program reviews; and data collected from current students, faculty and staff, alumni, and employers.

If data are already available through a database, time can be devoted to analysis and reporting. If, however, the data needed are not readily available and must be collected, the researcher must also choose the method: paper-pencil instrument, Web-based survey, personal interview, focus groups, or telephone survey. Resources (time, technology, person power, and expertise in areas such as Web survey development) may guide the decision. The list of instruments and publishers at the end of this chapter offers a starting point for guiding thoughts regarding data collection.

Especially if data are collected through a Web-based or paper-pencil survey, one of the most daunting tasks will be deciding if an institutionally-specific instrument should be created, or if a more generic instrument should be purchased from a publisher. Advantages and disadvantages must be weighed before reaching a decision. If an institutionally-specific instrument is developed, campus-specific issues can be addressed and will be less expensive (at least in dollars). In addition, when a committee of campus officials work together to articulate the goals and items to be included, a sense of commitment and excitement about the project is likely to occur. This can be an important indirect advantage to the development of an institutionally-specific questionnaire.

However, developing clear questions, designed in a user-friendly format, can be very time consuming and require pilot testing. In addition, institutionally-specific questionnaires require the developer to ensure a professional-looking form. This includes taking time to arrange for printing of the instrument and determining the procedure for scoring. In addition, institutionally-specific instruments require extensive commitments for reliability and validity checks. If a researcher/developer skips this important step of ensuring the instrument's reliability and validity, credibility for the instrument (as well as the researcher) may be jeopardized. This may increase chances for criticism and lower the overall investment in the project.

If the decision is made to purchase an instrument, the researcher must determine if the items are relevant for the population of students and investigate the instrument's advertised reliability and validity. It's always a good idea to pilot the instrument with a small group of students who are similar to those who will be surveyed. Many companies that offer assessment instruments also provide norms groups for inter-institutional comparisons. If there is not sufficient time, or the researcher does not have the ability to complete the written report, many companies also include the option of scoring and reporting services. Published instruments can be expensive (on average $3-$10 per student to purchase the instrument and scoring service), but can save time and effort that may be better devoted to other tasks. In addition, for some colleagues, a purchased instrument is the preferred choice simply because it 'looks good;' this increases its face validity and may likely add credibility to the assessment project.

3. Complete Data Collection and Analysis. Now that the researcher has carefully worked to understand the purpose, outline the goals, and determine the methods and measures, the fun begins! Just as there are advantages and disadvantages to purchased versus institutionally-specific instruments, there are also dilemmas about the efficacy of collection methods. Data collected through a mailed survey may enable the researcher to reach a larger population with minimal effort in survey distribution. Web-based data collection eliminates separate data entry and minimizes data coding errors, however, it can also offer a biased respondent population and can be intimidating to those students who do not feel comfortable using the computer. Surveys administered in a classroom setting will require the researcher schedule each session so that each classroom can be reached. Individual interviews or focus groups require extra effort prior to the interview or focus group to schedule the respondent or group as well as time needed to transcribe the discussion afterward. However, interviews and focus groups can offer high quality information that may not be possible from a Likert-type measure.

Once the data are collected, data analysis begins. During the planning stages, the researcher decides if someone on campus will complete the data entry or if the instruments will be sent to a company for scoring. Even if a summary report is received from the company, it is likely that the researcher will want to do additional analyses for the specific population. For example, an institution's division of nursing may want to know how majors in nursing responded to specific questions. Or, a dean may wish to know if there are differences in responses for commuter versus on-campus students. Such specific analyses are easily achieved through the use of a statistical package such as SPSS or SAS. Basic analyses, as well as the creation of charts and graphs, can also be achieved by using Excel or Access.

Data analysis is an exciting part of any assessment project! The research questions developed in step one should guide the analyses. A researcher should be inquisitive and analytical thinking about *what* the data means and *why* the responses follow certain patterns or trends.

4. Communicate the findings to the specific audience. Once the data analysis has been completed, the next step is to communicate the findings.

The intended audience may determine the method of communication, as well as the level of detail included in the report. Although a thorough set of statistical analyses must be completed to establish the findings, it is likely that the researcher will not want to include the detail of each statistical test.

In most instances, a written report will need to be prepared. An institutional research report is most likely to be read as an executive summary that includes highlights of the analysis. The researcher may wish to prepare a more detailed report that includes detail on each statistical analysis for those who are interested.

If an oral presentation has been planned, bulleted statements and a few charts on overhead transparencies or PowerPoint may be helpful. The researcher should be mindful of the following points when preparing an oral presentation:

- Think visually. How does the document look?

- Be careful of clutter. Include white space on each slide

- Use a font and type size that are readable. It is usually best to stay away from fancy scripts.

- Add clip art or other graphics for visual appeal, but be careful to not to allow them to overshadow the research.

- When possible, use color.

5. Obtain feedback, follow-up, redesign, and improve. A critical step in any assessment project is to use the findings to redesign and improve previous programs, services, or other processes. This feedback loop is the real key in making the institution's assessment plan a success. The feedback loop is also a critical element that many accreditation associations desire. The accreditation association for engineering, The Accreditation Board for Engineering & Technology (ABET), is now requiring (not recommending) that institutions show evidence of how previous assessment information is being incorporated in future programs, services or curriculum development.

Specific plans on how to incorporate feedback in future program planning are a challenge. If asked to contribute suggestions, the researcher will need to use creativity and analytical skills. Because each institution is unique, there are no cookie-cutter assessment designs that fit all departments or campuses. What may work in one department may not be the best solution for another. Similarly, definitions and methods for determining institutional effectiveness at one institution may not be the right combination at another. Familiarity with other campus or department models can be helpful as the researcher assists colleagues in planning follow-up and redesign for improvement.

A Note on Resource Planning

It's easy to remember that data collection via published surveys or professional focus group facilitators requires acquisition of funds for the purchase of the instrument or services. However, the researcher should also be certain to keep in mind the value in *total* resource planning. Once the necessary administrative support has been gained (consider the climate and political structures on campus), the researcher should be sure to delineate necessary personnel, materials, finances and time needed. Depending on the size of the project, personnel needs may include committee members to define the problem and/or develop questions for measurement, assistance with data collection, and/or consultation for statistical analyses. The researcher may likely need to clarify who will pay for survey instruments, materials (*e.g.,* envelopes, paper, Web space, incentive gifts) photocopying, and/or mailing. Financial needs include the purchase of materials, consultant time, or perhaps, if external grants are involved, a supplement to the researcher's office budget to compensate for time devoted to this project (see further discussion in the chapter on accountability).

The Value of a Model

Whenever possible, assessment plans should be guided through a theoretical model. A model encourages clarity regarding the purpose of the project and acts as a guide for developing the research plan. A model can help develop research questions as well as facilitate the planning of project design, data collection, and analysis. A plan will focus the researcher's energy and streamline the entire process, reducing the likelihood of spending unnecessary time on tangents. There are many good models from which to choose. For curricular assessment, theoretical models of cognitive development and moral reasoning may be effective (*i.e.,* Piaget, Kolhberg, Gilligan, Kitchener & King, Perry, Baxter-Magolda). For example, Bloom's *Taxonomy of Cognitive Domains* (Anderson & Krathwohl, 2001) offers an efficient way to approach the evaluation of student learning.

Several prominent researchers have developed models of student development and/or student retention and attrition. Pascarella and Terenzini (1991) offer a good, but brief, review of several relevant theories including Astin's I-E-O model and Theory of Involvement, Tinto's Theory of Student Departure, Spady's Model of the Undergraduate Dropout Process, Metzner and Bean's Model of Nontraditional Student Attrition, and Pascarella's Model for Assessing Student Change.

Examples of Instruments for Assessment Measures

Earlier in this chapter, issues to consider when making the decision to purchase or create an assessment instrument were discussed. Each assessment project will require making a decision each time, and will depend on your total set of resources (funding, time, and expertise). In many cases, the researcher may choose to purchase an instrument. For a brief description of many instruments and Web sites related to campus climate, see Schenkle, Snyder, and Bauer (1998). In addition, the following list of assessment instruments is by no means exhaustive, but may be helpful as the researcher formulates assessment plans. Detailed information about all instruments listed below can be easily obtained from such sources as the Mental Measurements Yearbook (Buros Institute, 1998), Tests in Print (Murphy, Impara, & Blake, 1999), the ERIC Assessment Web site, or from individual companies, such as American College Testing (ACT) or Educational Testing Service (ETS). In addition, the *NPEC Sourcebook on Assessment* (2000) reviews a variety of published instruments for the assessment of critical thinking, problem solving, and writing. A second *NPEC Sourcebook* reviewing instruments for quantitative reasoning, leadership, and diversity is currently in development and will be released in about 2003.

I. Student Assessment - Individual Instruments

General Education, Critical Thinking, Reasoning
Academic Profile
California Test of Critical Thinking
College BASE Academic Subjects Examination
Collegiate Assessment of Academic Proficiency
Cornell Test of Critical Thinking
Critical Thinking Assessment Battery
Defining Issues Test
Epistemology Questionnaire
Measure of Intellectual Development
Measure of Epistemological Reasoning
Reasoning About Current Issues
Reflective Judgment Interview
Tasks in Critical Thinking
Watson-Glaser Critical Thinking Appraisal

Measures of Subject Knowledge and/or Proficiency
e.g., National Chemistry Exam, Engineering, National Teacher Certification Exam,
Computer Technician Certification, Nursing Certification

Student Satisfaction, Attitudes and College Experiences
Student Opinion Survey
Freshman Needs Survey
College Student Experiences Survey (2 & 4yr versions)
College Student Expectations Survey
IDEA Course Evaluation Form (Kansas State University)
National Survey of Student Engagement
Noel-Levitz Satisfaction Inventory
Student Information Form
Your First Year College Survey

Campus Climate
Academic Setting Evaluation Questionnaire (for faculty)

Core Alcohol & Drug Use Survey

Harvard College Alcohol Study

Institutionally-specific Diversity Surveys including University of Delaware, University of Minnesota, Villanova University, Jacksonville State University

Institutionally-specific Employee Satisfaction Surveys including University of Delaware, Connecticut State University System, Cornell University, University of Iowa, University of Pittsburgh

Institutionally-specific Academic Advising Surveys

UCLA Diversity Surveys (Student, Faculty & Staff)

Withdrawing/Nonreturning Student Survey

Alumni

Alumni Outcomes Survey

National Center for Higher Education Management Systems (NCHEMS) Comprehensive Alumni Assessment Survey

NCHEMS Long-Term Alumni Questionnaire

NCHEMS Recent Alumni Questionnaire

Many institutionally-specific including State University of New York Albany, University of Delaware, University of North Carolina, Prince George's Community College, University of Pittsburgh

Institution

Institutional Goals Inventory

University Residence Environment Scale

Institutional Performance Survey

National Study of Instructional Costs and Productivity

II. Helpful Web sites

American College Testing Program, Inc. (ACT) - http://www.act.org

American Association for Higher Education (AAHE) http://www.aahe.org

Association for Institutional Research (AIR) - http://www.airweb.org

Center for Postsecondary Planning and Research (CSEQ, CSXQ, NSSE) - http://www.indiana.edu/~educ/pprcenter.html

ERIC/AE Assessment Clearinghouse - http://ericae2.educ.cua.edu

ERIC Clearinghouse for Community Colleges http://www.gse.ecla.edu/ERIC/welcome.html

ERIC Clearinghouse for Higher Education - http://www.gwu.edu/~eriche

Educational Testing Service (ETS) - http://www.ets.org

National Center for Higher Education Management Systems (NCHEMS)
http://www.nchems.com

National Survey of Student Engagement (NSSE)
http://www.indiana.edu/~nsse

Student Affairs Related Outcomes Instruments (SARTA)
http://isu.indstate.edu/wbarratt/dragon/ix/sa-indx.htm

UCLA Higher Education Research Institute
http://www.gseis.ucla.edu/heri

USA Group Noel-Levitz - http://www.usagroup.com/noelevtz/main.htm

III. Institutions with Assessment Plans Detailed on the Web
See listings maintained at:
North Carolina State University (this site is loaded with much good information) http://www2.acs.ncsu.edu/UPA/assmt/resource.htm

University of Missouri, Rolla
http://www.umr.edu/~assess/other/instass.html

References

Anderson, L. W. & Krathwohl, D. R. (2001). A taxonomy for learning, teaching, and assessing: A revision of Bloom's taxonomy of educational objectives. New York, NY: Longman.

American Association for Higher Education (AAHE). Definitions of assessment. Retrieved June, 2002 at: http://www.aahe.org/assessment/ assess_faq.htm#define.

Banta, T. W., Lund, J. P., Black, K. E., & Oberlander, F. W. (1996). Assessment in practice: Putting principles to work on college campuses. San Francisco, CA: Jossey-Bass.

Bauer, K. W., & Volkwein, J. F. (2000). Responding to Accreditation and Assessment on your Campus: Planning Steps and Strategies. Workshop presented at the Society for College and University Planning, July 2000, Atlanta, GA.

Boyer, C. M.& Ewell, P. T. (1988). State-based approaches to assessment in undergraduate education: A glossary and selected references. Denver, CO: Education Commission of the States.

Buros, O. K. (1998). The mental measurements yearbook. 13th edition. Highland Park, NJ: Gryphon Press.

Chickering, A. W. & Gamson, Z. F (1987). The seven principles of good practice in education. Originally published by the American Assessment for Higher Education. Reprinted by the Johnson Foundation, Inc., Racine, WI.

Erwin, T. D. (2000). The NPEC sourcebook on assessment, volume 1: Definitions and Assessment methods for critical thinking, problem-solving, and writing. National Postsecondary Education Cooperative Working Group on Student Outcomes Panel on Cognitive Outcomes. Retrieved June, 2002 at: http://nces.ed.gov/spider/webspider/2000195.shtml.

Erwin, T. D. (1991). Assessing student learning and development. San Francisco, CA: Jossey-Bass.

Harris, D., & Bell, C. (1986). Evaluating and assessing for learning. Kogan Page, London, England.

Gray, P. J. & Banta, T. W. (Eds.) (1997). New Directions for Higher Education: No. 100. The campus-level impact of assessment: Progress, problems, and possibilities. San Francisco, CA: Jossey-Bass.

Murphy, L. L, Impara, J. C. & Blake, B.S. (Eds.)(1999). Tests in print. Lincoln, NE: University of Nebraska Press.

Pascarella E. & Terenzini, P. T. (1991). How college affects students. San Francisco. CA: Jossey-Bass.

Schenkle, C. W., Snyder, R. S. & Bauer, K. W, (1998). In Bauer, K.W. (ed.) New Directions for Institutional Research: No. 98. Campus climate: Understanding the critical components of today's colleges and universities. San Francisco, CA: Jossey-Bass.

Suskie, L. (2000). Fair Assessment Practices. AAHE Bulletin, 52 (9), (pp. 7-9).

Upcraft, M. L. & Schuh, J. H. (1995). Assessment in student affairs: A guide for practitioners. San Francisco, CA: Jossey-Bass.

Chapter 3
Describing Faculty Activity and Productivity
for Multiple Audiences

Michael F. Middaugh
Heather Kelly Isaacs
University of Delaware

Introduction

The February 2, 2001, issue of *The Chronicle of Higher Education* contained an article titled "It's 10 am: Do You Know Where Your Professors Are?" (Wilson, 2001, pp. A10-A12) The article describes the evolution of a series of recommendations from a faculty committee at Boston University aimed at making faculty more accountable. The recommendations require that faculty be present in their offices a minimum of four days per week; that professors who are less productive in scholarly activity should do more teaching and service; and that if a faculty member cannot prove that he/she is productive, his or her employment status should be reduced to part time. Needless to say, the recommendations have resulted in a firestorm at Boston University. A Spanish professor was quoted saying, "I don't get paid for hanging around my office. I get pay increases for preparing for classes and because I publish books and articles and reviews" (Wilson, p. 10). The article goes on to say that: "It's not unusual for professors in English, history, modern languages, political science, and philosophy, for example, to come to campus only two or three days a week. The rest of the time professors spend writing at home or conducting research in libraries, archives, and museums – both local and afar. That's true not only for B.U. professors, but for those at research universities across the country" (Wilson, p.11). The faculty mentioned in this article imply that much of their scholarly activity takes place outside the classroom. However, the general feeling of those holding faculty accountable is that faculty should focus on teaching and time spent in the classroom and on campus.

The fact that the lead article in an issue of *The Chronicle* should focus on the controversial issue of how much time faculty spend in the classroom and how much time they spend on non-instructional activity is not at all surprising. Controversy has been building for years and is due, in no small measure, to self-inflicted wounds from higher education itself. The Boston University controversy is simply a microcosm of a larger dilemma in higher education. While the various facets of faculty activity at colleges and universities may be frequently discussed, there are few postsecondary institutions in America that **know** how faculty spend their time. Often faculty activity cannot be readily described in terms of concrete, tangible outputs from those activities. For example, the primary responsibility of teaching for faculty is not as simple as the act of teaching inside a classroom. Faculty members spend considerable

24

amounts of time preparing for their courses, assessing both their students and courses, and interacting with students outside of the classroom.

In 1999, Robert Zemsky of the University of Pennsylvania and William Massy of Stanford University asked faculty at nine institutions to comment on their instructional practices. The focus of the study was on how faculty planned their courses, prepared and administered their courses, assessed student performance, and interacted with students outside of class prior to the academic term, during the term, and at the end of the term. The faculty represented three private research universities, three private liberal arts colleges, and three public research or comprehensive universities. Overall, it was found that the time spent on the activities necessary to teach an undergraduate course were similar regardless of institution type. It is the general absence of the type of faculty productivity information discussed here that feeds mistrust of faculty, and the need to somehow hold them "accountable" by requiring their physical presence in the office four days a week.

This chapter represents a condensed version of arguments originally made in the recently published book, *Understanding Faculty Productivity: Standards and Benchmarks for Colleges and Universities* (Middaugh, 2001). The arguments are as follows:

- The dimensions of faculty activity are "knowable" and described in concrete terms that are easily understood;

- Higher education has done an abysmal job of translating what they "know" about faculty activity into a language that is understood both inside and outside of academe;

- Different audiences require different levels of complexity in describing faculty activity.

Whether at a major research university or a local community college, faculty, to one extent or another, engage in three types of activity: teaching (including course preparation, student and course assessment, academic advising, etc.), research, and service (including faculty governance, committee work, etc.). This has been demonstrated over time through a number of data sources. Perhaps the most consistent and reliable of these data sources is the *National Study of Postsecondary Faculty* (NSOPF), which is administered by the U.S. Department of Education at regular intervals to statistically weighted samples of faculty at colleges and universities throughout the United States. Table 1 looks at data from the two most recent NSOPF reports, which detail information from the 1987 and 1992 survey administrations. A third data collection is underway at this writing.

The data in Table 1 are remarkably consistent over time and attest to workload patterns that one might hypothesize across Carnegie institutional classifications. Faculty at research institutions spend roughly 40 percent of their time in teaching activity, another 33 percent in research, and the remainder in service and other forms of professional activity. Faculty at doctoral universities spend just under 50 percent of their time teaching, about 25 percent of their time in research, and the remainder in other activity. As one might expect, given their teaching mission, the proportion of time spent in teaching increases to about 60 percent at comprehensive and baccalaureate institutions, and increases to about 70 percent at two-year colleges. What is interesting is that faculty at comprehensive and baccalaureate institutions report spending 10

Table 1
Allocation of Time, by Function for Full-Time Instructional Faculty and Staff, by Type and Control of Institution: Fall 1987 and Fall 1992

Type and Control of Institution and Year	Full-Time Instructional Faculty and Staff	Percentage of Time Spent			
		Teaching Activities	Research Activities	Administrative Activities	Other Activities
1992					
All Institutions [1]	528,261	54.4	17.6	13.1	14.7
Public Research	107,358	40.4	31.5	12.9	15.2
Private Research	32,164	34.6	35.3	12.8	16.8
Public Doctoral [2]	52,808	46.8	23.8	13.2	16.1
Private Doctoral [2]	28,684	44.5	21.7	15.7	18.1
Public Comprehensive	94,477	60.2	14.0	12.0	13.7
Private Comprehensive	38,561	59.5	11.8	14.6	13.8
Private Liberal Arts	38,052	63.5	9.6	14.7	11.8
Public 2-Year	109,957	68.7	4.5	12.0	14.6
Other [3]	26,200	60.8	10.7	14.9	13.5
1987					
All Institutions [1]	515,139	57.1	17.3	13.2	12.5
Public Research	102,115	43.6	30.1	13.9	12.3
Private Research	41,574	42.1	30.6	13.2	14.2
Public Doctoral [2]	56,294	47.8	22.8	14.7	14.7
Private Doctoral [2]	25,065	41.1	26.4	12.8	19.6
Public Comprehensive	97,131	63.5	12.3	12.8	11.4
Private Comprehensive	36,842	63.7	11.2	14.2	11.0
Private Liberal Arts	38,446	66.8	10.5	13.8	9.0
Public 2-Year	96,144	73.3	4.2	10.9	11.6
Other [3]	21,528	63.6	8.8	15.2	12.5

[1] All accredited, nonproporietary U.S. postsecondary institutions that grant a 2-year (A.A.) or higher degree and whose accreditation at that higher education level is recognized by the U.S. Department of Education.

[2] Includes institutions classified by the Carnegie Foundation as specialized medical schools.

[3] Public liberal arts, private 2-year, and religious and other specialized institutions, except medical.

SOURCE: U.S. Department of Education, National Center for Education Statistics, 1993 and 1988 National Survey of Postsecondary Faculty, "Faculty Survey."

percent of their time in research, and while research is a vital component of scholarship, in theory it is not a component of promotion and tenure decisions at those institutions.

The time allocation patterns for American faculty described in Table 1 would surprise few in higher education. It is a commonly accepted academic tradition that faculty will construct their activity around the three pillars of teaching, research, and service to the institution and to the community. Because of the familiarity with the nature of faculty work within the Academy, the language for describing what faculty do is clouded with complacency. Colleges and universities assume that if they describe faculty activity in terms of percentage of time spent performing certain functions (i.e., the coin of the realm for typical "effort reports"), that description would suffice. Indeed, many colleges do, in fact, describe faculty work precisely in terms of the data array in Table 1.

Consider the following passage from the 1996 edition of *U.S. News and World Report's America's Best Colleges,* which describes the underlying causes of tuition increases during the 1990s:

> For their part, most colleges blame spiraling tuition on an assortment of off-campus scapegoats – congressional budget cutters, stingy state legislatures, government regulators and parents who demand ever more costly student health and recreational services. Rarely mentioned are the on-campus causes of the tuition crisis: declining teaching loads, non-productive research, ballooning financial aid programs, bloated administrative hierarchies, 'celebrity' salaries for professional stars, and inflated course offerings. If colleges and universities were rated on their overall financial acumen, most would be lucky to escape with a passing grade. (pp. 91-92)

Declining teaching loads? Non-productive research? One might infer from the percentages in Table 1 that, because the proportion of time spent teaching by faculty at research and doctoral universities declined somewhat from 1987 to 1992 and the proportion of time spent in research increased slightly, faculty taught less and did more research. However, the data in Table 1 do **not**, in fact, speak to either the volume of teaching done (i.e., teaching loads), or the quality of research being conducted in American colleges and universities. However, because postsecondary institutions have failed dismally in collecting quantitative and qualitative information that *credibly* describes faculty activities, sweeping generalizations such as those noted in the aforementioned *U.S. News and World Report* article are etched as gospel in the minds of parents and legislators.

Even inside higher education, where it is readily accepted that faculty engage in teaching, research, and service in meaningful ways, the means to describe faculty activities have been missing. Henry Rosovsky (1992), former Dean of the Faculty of Arts and Sciences at Harvard University, gives the following assessment:

27

From the point of view of a dean, two observations are in order. First, the dean has only the vaguest notion concerning what individuals teach. Second, the changes that have occurred [in faculty workloads, over time] were never authorized at the decanal level. At least that is what I believe and that is my main point. No chairman or group of science professors ever came to the dean to request a standard load of one-half course per year. No one ever requested a ruling concerning, for example, [workload] credit for shared courses. Change occurred through the use of *fait accompli*, i.e., creating facts. (p. 1B)

Two years earlier, Robert Zemsky of the University of Pennsylvania and William Massy of Stanford University, gave the following less-than-flattering portrait of faculty activity:

[The Academic Ratchet is…] A term to describe the steady, irreversible shift of faculty allegiance away from the goals of a given institution, toward those of an academic specialty. The ratchet denotes the advance of an entrepreneurial spirit among faculty nationwide, leading to an increased emphasis on research and publication, and on teaching one's specialty in favor of general introduction courses, often at the expense of coherence in an academic curriculum. Institutions seeking to enhance their own prestige may contribute to the ratchet by reducing faculty teaching and advising responsibilities across the board, thus enabling faculty to pursue their individual research and publication with fewer distractions. The academic ratchet raises an institution's costs, and it results in undergraduates paying more to attend institutions in which they receive less attention than in previous decades. (1990, p. 22)

The foregoing examples suggest that few, either inside higher education or outside, know precisely what faculty do, how much they do or how well they do it, and at what cost to the institution. The result has been a tidal wave of criticism directed at American higher education, with the gravest consequences coming in the form of state regulations concerning accountability, a number of which are wholly inappropriate and potentially damaging to colleges and universities. The Education Commission of the States surveyed 35 state governors on their views of higher education. All of the governors believed that colleges and universities should be more accountable and felt that there should be an increased emphasis on faculty productivity. Interestingly enough, only 32% of the governors surveyed believed that it is very important to important to maintain the present balance of faculty research, teaching load, and community service (Schmidt, 1998). While these calls for increased accountability may be partly because of the fact that the involvement of government officials in the realm of higher education has increased, as noted earlier, these consequences are really self-inflicted wounds on the part of American higher education. There is currently a demand for a language describing faculty activity that is:

- Understandable and credible for individuals outside of higher education who have a stake in what college and universities do and how those activities impact undergraduates, in particular.

- Useful and usable by provosts, deans, department chairs, and others interested in effectively and efficiently managing resources, both personnel and fiscal.

When asked what faculty do, whether the question is raised by a parent or a legislator, the most common type of response over time has been that faculty spend X percent of their time teaching, Y percent of their time doing research, and Z percent of their time engaged in either institutional or public service. Because faculty are not always present and visible on campus as they engage in the various facets of their activities, there is a growing skepticism as to the denominator in such descriptions of work. The prevailing assumption, as previously evidenced in the quotes from Zemsky and Massy, Rosovsky, and *U.S. News*, is that faculty are a mercenary lot, focused largely on entrepreneurial activity aimed at self aggrandizement, as opposed to the welfare of students, the college or university that employs them, and the larger society they are supposed to serve. Higher education's inability to respond to such latent assumptions with measurable, credible data has done little to quell the cynicism.

The data in Table 2 reflect the self-reported mean number of hours that faculty work each week, arrayed by Carnegie institution type. Unless the wholly unwarranted assumption that faculty are pathological liars is made, the data in Table 2 should be accepted at face value. Taking the data in Tables 1 and 2 collectively, it can be assumed that faculty spend significant blocks of time in teaching, research, and service. But this sort of response still does not tell us what faculty *do*.

Turning the Discussion Around

The central thesis of the book, *Understanding Faculty Productivity*, is that discussions of faculty activity have historically been in the terms just described: number of hours spent in certain functional areas. These are clearly *input* measures that in no way describe the products of faculty activity. If faculty activity is to be discussed in meaningful ways, those discussions must clearly be in terms of *outputs* (i.e., metrics that describe the outcomes of faculty activity). If the solution were that simple, the discussions might well have shifted in the appropriate direction years ago. The critical component in effecting this paradigm shift is the definition and articulation of appropriate outcomes measures that fully and adequately describe the broad spectrum of faculty activity, as well as their products. That definition and articulation has gained momentum only in recent years, and its evolution is the focus of *Understanding Faculty Productivity*.

Joint Commission on Accountability Reporting (JCAR)

During the mid-1990s, in response to external and internal criticism of the sort outlined earlier in this chapter, the presidents of colleges and universities

Table 2

Mean Number of Hours Worked by Full-Time Instructional Faculty and Staff, by Type and Control of Institution: Fall 1987 and Fall 1992

Type and Control of Institution and Year	Full-Time Instructional Faculty and Staff	Mean Hours Worked per Week
1992		
All Institutions [1]	528,261	52.5
Public Research	107,358	56.4
Private Research	32,164	57.6
Public Doctoral [2]	52,808	55.1
Private Doctoral [2]	28,684	53.4
Public Comprehensive	94,477	52.4
Private Comprehensive	38,561	51.9
Private Liberal Arts	38,052	52.5
Public 2-Year	109,957	46.9
Other [3]	26,200	49.0
1987		
All Institutions [1]	515,139	52.7
Public Research	102,115	56.8
Private Research	41,574	56.1
Public Doctoral [2]	56,294	54.7
Private Doctoral [2]	25,065	52.2
Public Comprehensive	97,131	52.7
Private Comprehensive	36,842	51.2
Private Liberal Arts	38,446	52.5
Public 2-Year	96,144	46.9
Other [3]	21,528	51.9

[1] All accredited, nonproporietary U.S. postsecondary institutions that grant a 2-year (A.A.) or higher degree and whose accreditation at that higher education level is recognized by the U.S. Department of Education.

[2] Includes institutions classified by the Carnegie Foundation as specialized medical schools.

[3] Public liberal arts, private 2-year, and religious and other specialized institutions, except medical.

SOURCE: U.S. Department of Education, National Center for Education Statistics, 1993 and 1988 National Survey of Postsecondary Faculty, "Faculty Survey."

throughout the nation sought a vehicle for effectively responding to such criticism. Three national organizations, the American Association of State Colleges and Universities (AASCU), the National Association of State Universities and Land Grant Colleges (NASULGC), and the American Association of Community Colleges (AACC) created the Joint Commission on Accountability Reporting (JCAR). JCAR was charged with the responsibility of developing tangible and credible measures that would describe the outcomes and products of higher education. The American Association of Independent Colleges and Universities (AAICU), the Washington-based organization representing private institutions in the United States, was invited to participate in JCAR but declined.

The Joint Commission was comprised of representative presidents from institutions within each of the Washington-based organizations. The presidents determined that the following four areas should be the focus of JCAR:

1. Placement rates and full-time employment in the field, following the completion of a higher education program or degree.

2. Graduation rates, persistence rates, licensure pass rates, and transfers of students.

3. Student charges and costs, underscoring the difference between "sticker price" (i.e., what an institution charges a student to attend), and "cost" (i.e., what an institution spends to educate that student).

4. Faculty activity.

The Joint Commission then appointed four technical work groups organized around each of the four measurement areas. The technical work groups were comprised of faculty, senior administrators in the areas of higher education management, academic affairs, and student affairs. In addition, each technical work group included a number of senior institutional researchers with acknowledged measurement expertise in the functional area of their work group.

The JCAR technical work groups were instructed to deliberate along a number of operating tenets:

- Data was to focus on outcomes or products;

- Metrics must be simple, clear, and easy to understand; and

- Target audience was parents, legislators, and others outside of higher education who lack a sophisticated understanding of how colleges and universities operate.

The rationale behind this approach was simple. Parents pay the tuition that institutions charge their children to attend; legislatures underwrite, at least in part, the cost of delivering an education. **What is the return on this investment?** Faculty engage in activities related to their employment at a college or university. As the result of those activities, do students progress through the institution with reasonable levels of success? Are they employable in positions related to their fields of study following graduation? Do they successfully acquire licenses and other professional credentials? Are they admitted to graduate schools in appropriate fields of study? The answers to these questions would prove that parents and legislators were receiving a tangible return from their investment.

It should be noted that the JCAR reporting conventions are not designed to be management tools for higher education administrators. Other initiatives during the 1990s emerged that successfully provided those tools. Instead, JCAR was intended to serve as a language for communicating with external publics about the work and products of higher education as returns on money invested by parents and government(s). In that regard, JCAR was remarkably successful.

JCAR reintroduced a measure for faculty activity that dated back to the mid-1970s: the *service month*. The service month reports how much time faculty spend on various activities that are a part of their contractual agreement. The service month acknowledges the fact that faculty do not spend September, October, and November exclusively engaged in teaching; December, January, and February exclusively engaged in research; and March, April, and May exclusively engaged in public service. The service month does not rely on self-reported faculty estimates of how their time is allocated between and among teaching, research, and service. Heretofore, these data had been greeted with cynicism and skepticism.

The JCAR Technical Work Group on Faculty Activity Reporting decided that the reporting convention would utilize the prospective faculty work program that is characteristically agreed upon by the faculty member and his/her department chair prior to the beginning of an academic year. This is not a whimsical appraisal of how time may, or may not, have been spent during the prior 12 months. Rather, it is a road map, a mutually codified agreement as to how a faculty member will spend time during the year and, in most instances, is a basis for faculty evaluation. The Technical Work Group certainly understood that the work program could, and often does, change during the course of an academic year. However, in their judgment, because the work agreement is a management tool for the department chair and the basis for institutional assessment of how faculty are expected to spend their time, it has far more credibility than self-reported data.

The measurement metrics for service months are quite straightforward. According to the *JCAR Technical Conventions Manual* (1996), a service month:

> …is a unit of work equivalent to one person working full-time for one calendar month and can be allocated by function (i.e., teaching, research, or service). For example, a full-time 12-month employee with half-time responsibility as a college's director of institutional research and half-time responsibility as a member of the mathematics faculty produces six administrative service months and six faculty service months in that year. In the case of those functioning solely as faculty, service months

can be distributed over the three categories of faculty work: teaching, research/scholarship, and service. Consider the full time, 9-month faculty member whose *assigned* (not self-reported) responsibilities include 50 percent teaching, 30 percent research, and 20 percent service. The service months for that individual would be distributed as follows: 4.5 months in teaching (i.e., 9 months multiplied by 50 percent); 2.7 months in research (i.e., 9 months multiplied by 30 percent); and 1.8 months in service activity (i.e., 9 months multiplied by 20 percent). (p. 7)

It is important to underscore that the service month is not synonymous with a calendar month. While a service month of service activity might well take place entirely within the calendar month of October, it might just as easily reflect 30 days of research activity spread out over several calendar months. Reporting faculty activity in terms of service months, as opposed to the traditional percentage of time metric, provides a more tangible assessment of how faculty are expected to spend their time during the academic year. To say that a faculty member spends 50 percent of his/her time teaching does not covey a sense of how much time that represents. Is it 50 percent of an eight-hour day or, is it 50 percent of a 40-hour week? On the other hand, if we know that a faculty member generates 4.5 service months from teaching, we can easily translate that into roughly 135 days out of the work year devoted exclusively to teaching activity.

The *service month* is the first nationally standardized output measure of faculty activity. While it is purely quantitative, and in no way speaks to the quality of what faculty do, it is nonetheless a step forward in that it provides a consistent, concrete measure of the volume of faculty activity at a given institution. That said, it is still a very limited measure. It speaks only to how much time is expected to be devoted to various functional activities as part of a faculty member's contractual assignment, in terms that anyone can readily understand. It does not speak to outcomes or products of those activities. It does, however, make clear to those outside of higher education that there is a clear expectation, on the part of both the faculty member and academic management, that the scope of the faculty member's duties will embrace more than just instruction. Clarity regarding this expectation is important to helping parents, legislators, and others come to terms with the reality of faculty life, as compared with traditional perceptions of faculty as strictly teachers.

JCAR helps to make some important correlations between process and output. It facilitates the understanding that faculty do not spend 100 percent of any given year engaged strictly in teaching. It does, however, provide a series of productivity measures for the time that is, in fact, spent on instructional activity. The effectiveness of faculty instructional activity is measured in terms of retention and graduation rates, for which JCAR also provides calculation conventions. Calculation conventions are also provided for the proportion of graduates finding curriculum related occupations, entering graduate school, passing licensure or certification exams, etc. The JCAR calculation and reporting conventions make the first serious attempt to tie faculty activity to the instructional products of higher education. One might well wish that JCAR had extended the process to include the products of research and service. However, because instruction was the focus of external criticism at the time, they limited their analysis to that realm. Other tools for examining the products of research and service will be discussed elsewhere in this chapter.

JCAR, for the first time, offered parents, taxpayers, legislators and other interested non-academicians a clear, unambiguous framework for understanding how faculty spend their time and, in the instance of instruction, how to measure the outputs of faculty activity. Interested readers should obtain and consult the primary JCAR publications, which are available from the American Association of State Colleges and Universities. These include the *JCAR Technical Conventions Manual*, which describes the overall JCAR framework and the calculation and reporting conventions associated with it, and *JCAR Faculty Assignment Reporting*, which provides a detailed framework for how to measure and describe faculty activity for those outside of higher education.

The *JCAR Faculty Assignment Reporting* (1997) manual includes the following paragraph:

> The purpose of this document is to give institutions a 'technical manual' approach to reporting strategies to describe what faculty are assigned to do, and which faculty members are teaching the students. The reporting calculations and conventions developed in this document, although useful for some internal planning or management purposes, are intended to provide information for external audiences, state legislators, budget officers and consumers. Those interested in analytical and reporting techniques specifically designed for internal management use are referred to the National Study of Instructional Costs and Productivity, housed at the University of Delaware…. (p. 5)

The National Study of Instructional Costs and Productivity, or "The Delaware Study," is an analytical tool and strategy for assessing the cost effectiveness of instructional resource deployment at the academic discipline level of analysis. The study grew out of specific measurements designed for just such assessments at one institution, then extended to other institutions to become the largest data sharing consortium directed at measuring instructional costs and productivity. The remainder of this chapter will describe the development of those institutional metrics and their evolution into the Delaware Study of Instructional Costs and Productivity.

Budget Support Data

In the late 1980s and early 1990s, the University of Delaware found itself in the midst of an economic recession that was enveloping the Mid-Atlantic States. This was compounded by poor financial decision-making at the institution that resulted in $13 million in recurring items being funded out of non-recurring revenues. It was clear to the new senior leadership that the University had to reduce expenditures, both in response to the recession and in order to balance the institution's budgets.

Approaching the issue of expenditure reductions, the University adopted a policy, in place at the present, that horizontal (i.e., across the board) budget cuts encourage pervasive mediocrity and are, therefore, unacceptable. Vertical cuts targeted at wasteful or non-essential programs are the appropriate course of action. The University initiated the expenditure reduction program by focusing on administrative functions during the first several years of cuts. However, it was evident that, at some point, academic programs would be affected. While it is relatively easy to measure fiscal excess and/or irrelevance in administrative units, it is far more difficult to do so in academic units. Appropriate measures of cost and productivity were clearly essential. Those measures needed to be clear and unambiguous and accepted and used by all sectors within the University community.

The Office of Institutional Research and Planning at the University of Delaware was charged with responsibility of developing these measures, in conjunction with academic units at the institution. The measures had to underpin management decisions (i.e., financial and personnel reductions and reallocations). Consequently, the measures had to be embraced and accepted by deans, department chairs, members of the faculty senate, as well as the directors of the budget and institutional research offices.

Table 3 depicts a page from the University's Budget Support Notebooks. In this instance, the page is from an undergraduate humanities department within the College of Arts and Science. In negotiating with deans and department chairs concerning which measures should drive productivity data, some compromise was necessary. This compromise is best illustrated by the first two measures in Table 3: "FTE Majors" and "Degrees Granted." These are traditional views of "productivity," and deans and chairs wanted to see these figures. On the other hand, there are a few more misleading measures when examining instructional productivity. In the first instance, FTE Majors is nothing more than a headcount (the total of part-time students, divided by three, and added to full-time students). It is a measure of student preference for majoring in a discipline and has little to do with teaching activity within that discipline. The same can be said for degrees granted; if there are few majors, there will be few degrees granted, as evidenced in the department in Table 3, Part A. If these were the *only* productivity measures used for making resource allocation and reallocation decisions, the department in Table 3 would likely be closed.

However, better measures do exist for assessing instructional productivity. Returning to Part A of Table 3, it is evident that faculty in this department teach some 7,000+ student credit hours per semester. Undergraduates carry semester loads of approximately 15 credit hours. Approximately 40 majors, in this department, account for less than 600 of those student credit hours. There clearly is considerable teaching activity that goes well beyond 40 majors, or 20 degrees granted.

The Budget Support notebooks provide two additional key indicators related to the productivity of this department. The "Percent of Credit Hours Taught by Faculty on Appointment" is a University of Delaware term for the proportion of student credit hours that are being taught by tenured and tenure track faculty, those in whom the institution has the greatest investment. In this department, the proportion averages around 80 percent. This is important information to have at a time when tenured and tenure track faculty are coming increasingly under fire for pursuing their research and publishing interests at the expense of undergraduate instruction. In addition, this statistic provides evidence to counter any argument that students are being taught primarily by teaching assistants or instructors.

The other key indicator is "Percent of Student Credit Hours Consumed by Non-Majors." Not surprisingly, the proportion for this department is 97 to 98 percent. Because this is a humanities department, and its courses are critical to satisfying general education requirements at the University, this indicator suggests that any policy that significantly reduced the teaching capability of this department would have a strongly adverse effect on the ability of non-majors to fulfill those general education requirements. It is data such as these, not headcount majors or degrees granted, that are crucial to understanding the instructional dynamics of an academic department or program.

The "FTE Students Taught" measure in Table 3 is very different from FTE majors. It is a direct measure of teaching activity. It assumes that undergraduates typically carry a semester load of 15 hours, while graduate students carry 9, and uses those as divisors for student credit hours taught. It translates student credit hours into full-time equivalent students; both can be used with "FTE Faculty" to arrive at two very useful teaching productivity ratios: "Student Credit Hours Taught per FTE Faculty" and "FTE Students Taught per FTE Faculty." The latter is a true student faculty ratio and is very useful in comparing teaching loads between and among departments. It is clearly influenced by the "undergraduateness" or "graduateness" of a department as reflected in the calculation's divisors; therefore it is a more sensitive measure than simply student credit hours taught per FTE faculty.

Part B of The Budget Support Data combines teaching load information with expenditure data to provide a sense of the cost of instruction in a department or program. Data on externally funded or separately budgeted research and public service activity is also provided as contextual information for looking at cost data, as will be described shortly. Looking at the humanities department in Part B of Table 3, not surprisingly, there is little in the way of externally funded research or service activity. External funding from sources such as the National Endowment for the Humanities, or the National Endowment for the Arts, have all but ceased in recent years.

Table 3
Budget Support Data

				College of Arts and Science Department X		
1995-96 Through 1997-98						
A. TEACHING WORKLOAD DATA						
	FALL 1995	**FALL 1996**	**FALL 1997**	**SPRING 1996**	**SPRING 1997**	**SPRING 1998**
FTE MAJORS						
Undergraduate	32	38	31	40	38	40
Graduate	0	0	0	0	0	0
Total	32	38	31	40	38	40
DEGREES GRANTED						
Bachelor's	-----	-----	-----	20	19	19
Master's	-----	-----	-----	0	0	0
Doctorate	-----	-----	-----	0	0	0
Total	-----	-----	-----	20	19	19
STUDENT CREDIT HOURS						
Lower Division	7,554	6,246	5,472	6,399	4,518	6,156
Upper Division	719	826	638	946	1,159	951
Graduate	195	183	153	192	195	276
Total	8,468	7,255	6,263	7,537	5,872	7,383
% Credit Hours Taught by Faculty on Appointment	77%	77%	81%	75%	82%	91%
% Credit Hours Taught by Supplemental Faculty	23%	23%	19%	25%	18%	9%
% Credit Hours Consumed by Non-Majors	98%	97%	98%	96%	98%	97%
FTE STUDENTS TAUGHT						
Lower Division	504	416	356	427	301	410
Upper Division	48	48	43	63	77	63
Graduate	22	20	17	21	22	31
Total	574	484	425	511	400	504
FTE FACULTY						
Department Chair	1.0	1.0	1.0	1.0	1.0	1.0
Faculty on Appointment	15.0	15.0	16.0	14.0	15.0	15.0
Supplemental Faculty	1.8	1.5	1.0	1.8	1.0	0.8
Total	17.8	17.5	18.0	16.8	17.0	16.8
WORKLOAD RATIOS						
Student Credit Hrs./FTE Faculty	477.1	408.9	347.9	450.0	345.4	440.8
FTE Students Taught/FTE Faculty	32.3	27.7	23.6	30.5	23.5	30.1

Table 3 (continued)
Budget Support Data

B. FISCAL DATA			
	FY 1996 ($)	FY 1997 ($)	FY 1998 ($)
RESEARCH AND SERVICE			
Research Expenditures	0	0	5,151
Public Service Expenditures	0	0	0
Total Sponsored Research/Service	0	0	5,151
Sponsored Funds/FTE Fac. on Appointment	0	0	312
COST OF INSTRUCTION			
Direct Instructional Expenditures	1,068,946	1,060,975	1,147,927
Direct Expense/Student Credit Hour	67	81	84
Direct Expense/FTE Student Taught	1,830	2,188	1,231
REVENUE MEASURES			
Earned Income from Instruction	4,561,245	3,960,208	4,366,720
Earned Income/Direct Instructional Expense	4.27	3.73	3.82

The cost of instruction in Part B of Table 3 refers to the *direct* expenditures for instruction during any given fiscal year. This information is detailed by student credit hour and FTE students taught.

All colleges and universities (virtually every postsecondary institution in the United States) that subscribe to generally accepted accounting principles use a specific convention when assigning a transaction number to each and every expenditure at the institution. Embedded in that transaction number is an object code that describes what the money is being spent for (i.e., salaries, travel, supplies, etc.) and a function code that describes the purpose for which it is being spent (i.e., teaching, research, public service, institutional support, etc.).

Table 4 is a simple matrix developed by the Office of Institutional Research and Planning at the University of Delaware as backup information for the budget support notebooks. It arrays fiscal year expenditures by object and by function for each academic department for which we generate budget support data. Note that the "bottom line" (i.e., total expenditures for the instruction function for this department) is $1,141,927. This is precisely the same number that appears in the "Total Direct Instructional Expenditures" field in Fiscal Year 1998 in Part B of Table 3. The data in Table 4 indicate to the dean or department chair exactly how these funds were spent. The Office of Institutional Research and Planning at the University of Delaware has a close working relationship with the Budget Office. On those rare occasions when the matrix data such as those in Table 4 are challenged, the Budget Office will generate a transaction-by-transaction report for the questioning department. This report invariably matches, to the penny, the number reported in the Budget Support Notebook and supporting matrix.

Table 4
Departmental Expenditures, by Object and by Function:
Fiscal Year 1998
Undergraduate Department in Humanities

	Instruction (01-08)	Departmental Research (09)	Org. Activity Educ. Depts. (10)	Research (21-39)	Public Service (41-43)	Academic Support (51-56)
Expenditures						
Salaries						
Professionals	26,509	0	0	0	0	0
Faculty						
Full-Time (Including Dept. Chair)	977,775	0	0	0	0	0
Part-Time (Including Overload)	33,968	0	0	0	0	0
Graduate Students	0	0	0	0	0	0
Post Doctoral Fellows	0	0	0	2,591	0	0
Tuition/Scholarship	0	0	0	0	0	0
Salaried/Hourly Staff	62,224	0	0	0	0	0
Fringe Benefits	0	0	0	0	0	0
Subtotal	1,100,476	0	0	2,591	0	0
Support						
Miscellaneous Wages	3,721	160	0	0	0	0
Travel	9,045	6,645	0	0	0	0
Supplies and Expenses	18,315	6,860	0	2,500	0	0
Occupancy and Maintenance	1,287	0	0	0	0	0
Equipment	0	0	0	0	0	0
Other Expenses	9,083	0	0	0	0	0
Credits and Transfers	0	0	0	0	0	0
Subtotal	41,451	13,665	0	2,560	0	0
TOTAL EXPENDITURES	1,141,927	13,665	0	5,151	0	0

This is one additional means of establishing the veracity and credibility of the data.

As noted, the expenditure data in the Budget Support Notebook reflect direct expenses. The decision was made to look at direct expense, as opposed to full cost, because the definitional components of direct expenses are clear and unambiguous. Derived from accounting definitions established by the National Association of Collegiate and University Business Officers (NACUBO), the definition for a direct instructional expense is the same for physics as for anthropology or for art. The same is not true for indirect expenses. Indirect cost formulae vary by discipline and by funding source for those units with external contract or grant activity. Rather than get into contentious and non-productive debates over whose indirect cost formula is most accurate, the decision was made at the University of Delaware (and, as will be seen shortly, ratified at some 300-plus colleges and universities across the country) to focus on direct expenditure data with all of its clarity and precision.

With the direct instructional expenditure data found in Part B of Table 3, it is possible to use that figure as the numerator in two important calculations. If the direct instructional expenditures are divided by total student credit hours taught, or by FTE students taught as defined earlier, two highly useful cost ratios emerge: direct expense per student credit hour taught and direct expense per FTE student taught. As previously noted, the direct expense per credit hour taught is not sensitive to whether it is an undergraduate or graduate credit hour; on the other hand, the FTE students taught is a function of the relative "undergraduateness" or "graduateness" of instruction.

Table 3 provides an interesting portrait of a primarily undergraduate unit whose mission is largely a teaching mission. The workload ratios of between 345 and 475 student credit hours taught per FTE faculty each term, and a 25 to 30:1 student faculty ratio, are among the highest workload ratios at the University. Because there is little research or service activity, it would be reasonable to expect a higher volume of teaching and, concomitantly, lower instructional costs. All of the Budget Support data line up to support these assumptions.

Table 5 displays budget support data for a physical science department with a graduate research orientation. The FTE majors and degrees granted data in Part A of Table 5 underscore the graduate nature of this department. Looking at the workload ratios, however, the data are in stark contrast to the humanities department. The workload ratios indicate roughly 30 student credit hours taught per faculty and a 3:1 student faculty ratio. If these were the only indicators used, they would suggest that very little teaching occurs. The cost of instruction ratios in Part B of Table 5, over $1,000 per student credit hour taught and over $10,000 per FTE student taught, might be a stimulus to close the department.

These data underscore the importance of a full picture. In this instance, the full picture includes the expenditure data for separately budgeted research and service. This is a graduate department in the physical sciences and not all of the graduate level instruction in scientific disciplines can be measured in terms of student credit hours taught. Indeed, most of the instruction occurs in the laboratory, in terms of the interaction between a research faculty member and his/her graduate research assistant. Does research occur in this department? Separately budgeted research/service expenditures, on the order of more than a quarter million dollars per faculty member, suggest that considerable research is occurring and that these expenditures are likely supporting the graduate students in the laboratory.

The Budget Support Notebooks have helped underscore the fact that there are different types of faculty productivity across different departments at the University. Each form of productivity, be it teaching, research or service, is essential to the University, as a total entity, and in achieving the University's mission. Another type of data further underscores the diversity of academic

Table 5
Budget Support Data

					College of Marine Studies Department X		
1996-97 Through 1998-99							
A. TEACHING WORKLOAD DATA							

	FALL 1996	FALL 1997	FALL 1998	SPRING 1997	SPRING 1998	SPRING 1999
FTE MAJORS						
Undergraduate	0	0	0	0	0	0
Graduate	75	74	94	72	73	87
Total	75	74	94	72	73	87
DEGREES GRANTED						
Bachelor's	-----	-----	-----	0	0	0
Master's	-----	-----	-----	15	14	15
Doctorate	-----	-----	-----	9	7	9
Total	-----	-----	-----	24	21	24
STUDENT CREDIT HOURS						
Lower Division	210	156	216	0	0	0
Upper Division	10	43	46	70	12	31
Graduate	848	668	759	740	718	696
Total	1,068	867	1,021	810	730	727
% Credit Hours Taught by Faculty on Appointment	96%	96%	95%	95%	95%	92%
% Credit Hours Taught by Supplemental Faculty	4%	4%	5%	5%	5%	8%
% Credit Hours Consumed by Non-Majors	3%	2%	3%	0%	0%	0%
FTE STUDENTS TAUGHT						
Lower Division	14	10	14	0	0	0
Upper Division	1	3	3	5	1	2
Graduate	94	74	84	82	80	77
Total	109	87	101	87	81	79
FTE FACULTY						
Department Chair	0.0	0.0	0.0	0.0	0.0	0.0
Faculty on Appointment	31.0	30.8	28.8	31.0	29.8	27.8
Supplemental Faculty	0.3	0.3	0.3	0.5	0.3	0.3
Total	31.3	31.1	29.1	31.5	30.1	28.1
WORKLOAD RATIOS						
Student Credit Hrs./FTE Faculty	34.1	27.9	35.0	25.7	24.2	25.9
FTE Students Taught/FTE Faculty	3.5	2.8	3.5	2.8	2.7	2.8

B. FISCAL DATA

	FY 1997 ($)	FY 1998 ($)	FY 1999 ($)
RESEARCH AND SERVICE			
Research Expenditures	7,205,881	6,170,077	6,829,638
Public Service Expenditures	959,191	1,078,595	1,085,352
Total Sponsored Research/Service	8,165,072	7,248,672	7,914,990
Sponsored Funds/FTE Fac. On Appointment	263,389	239,072	279,484
COST OF INSTRUCTION			
Direct Instructional Expenditures	1,627,935	1,760,309	2,329,922
Direct Expense/Student Credit Hour	867	1,102	1,333
Direct Expense/FTE Student Taught	8,316	10,475	12,858
REVENUE MEASURES			
Earned Income from Instruction	570,912	511,040	578,588
Earned Income/Direct Instructional Expense	0.35	0.29	0.25

department types: the "income to expense ratio." This is the final component of the budget support data.

The income to expense ratio looks at revenue from teaching activity, comparing it with direct expenditures for teaching activity. Because most institutions, including the University of Delaware, book tuition centrally and do not actually measure tuition as a function of teaching activity, a proxy measure is needed. This is even more important for public institutions, which charge differential tuition rates to resident and non-resident students. The simplest solution is the following calculation:

1. Determine total tuition revenue at a college or university for a given fiscal year by looking at the institutional financial statement.

2. Divide total tuition revenue by the total number of student credit hours taught at the institution during the same fiscal year.

3. The quotient is a "Per Student Credit Hour" tuition revenue unit that is then multiplied by the total number of student credit hours taught at the academic department level during that same fiscal year. The result is "Earned Income From Instruction" (i.e., tuition revenue generated by teaching activity in that department).

In a unit, such as the humanities department in Table 3, with high volume instruction and a relatively low cost pedagogical delivery system (primarily large classroom lectures), the earned income from instruction will be relatively high. When compared to expenses, it will yield a ratio that annually approaches 4.0 (i.e., revenues four times the amount of expenses). On the other hand, a graduate physical science department, such as that in Table 5, with low student credit hour generation (and low earned income from instruction), coupled with high instructional expenses related to the salaries of faculty and the equipment intensive nature of such disciplines, result in income to expense ratios of well under 1.0. If viewed in isolation, this would suggest that this department cannot cover its expenses and would be an ideal candidate for closure. However, as noted earlier, there are contextual data in the research and service information. The department in Table 5 is clearly a major component of the University's research mission. Moreover, although not earned income from instruction, recovered indirect costs from research activity are very real revenues that go into the University's general fund. Once again, the data illustrate different views of faculty productivity related to different parts of the University's overall mission.

These data have been extremely useful in helping the University of Delaware to make appropriate comparisons between and among its own academic departments related to faculty productivity within the context of the complex institutional mission. These data are also useful in helping to look for trend information related to cost and productivity over time. In addition, they are also essential ingredients in resource allocation and reallocation decisions.

However, the relative cost and productivity of a given academic department or program can only be known by comparing it with comparable departments or programs at other institutions. Inter-institutional comparative data is the final ingredient in looking at faculty productivity. Fortunately, a tool exists for making such comparisons.

The Delaware Study of Instructional Costs and Productivity

When University of Delaware President David P. Roselle arrived at the institution in 1990, he was quite pleased with the management information available to him in the Budget Support Notebooks. He indicated to the Office of Institutional Research and Planning that the data would be even more useful if they were cast in the context of departments and programs at institutions that are actual peers, as well as institutions to which the University aspires to be peers. Out of that comment, the Delaware Study of Instructional Costs and Productivity was born. Begun in 1992, with a participant pool of 86 institutions, the Delaware Study has grown into a major national data sharing consortium of well over 300 institutions. It annually collects detailed information on teaching loads, by faculty type, direct instructional expenses, and externally or separately budgeted scholarship activity, all at the level of the academic discipline. Readers interested in a detailed description of the Delaware Study, including data definitions, calculation conventions, and a copy of the data collection protocol are directed to the Delaware Study link on the Institutional Research and Planning Web site at http://www.udel.edu/IR.

For purposes of this discussion, the focus will be on how Delaware Study data can be used in framing discussions about enhancing faculty productivity. While the Delaware Study has the capability of looking at the full range of activity for four categories of faculty – tenured and tenure eligible; full time non-tenure eligible; supplemental/adjunct; and graduate teaching assistants – the Office of Academic Affairs at the University of Delaware opts to focus on the tenured and tenure eligible faculty. The underlying reasons for this choice are as follows:

1. Faculty salaries account for, on average, between 85 and 90 percent of direct instructional expenditures in any given academic discipline. Because tenured and tenure track faculty tend to be paid better than non-tenure eligible faculty, they are the major cost drivers within the salary component of direct instructional expenses.

2. Tenured faculty are "fixed costs." Once faculty are tenured, they are with the institution until retirement, resignation, or death. Hence, it makes good business sense to look at the productivity return from this fixed asset.

3. They are the most visible faculty category. No newspaper has ever written an editorial or investigative reporting piece wondering about the teaching loads of non-tenure eligible or adjunct faculty. Tenured faculty tend to be the primary target of external criticism of higher

Figure 1
University of Delaware Academic Benchmarking
Large Department in Humanities

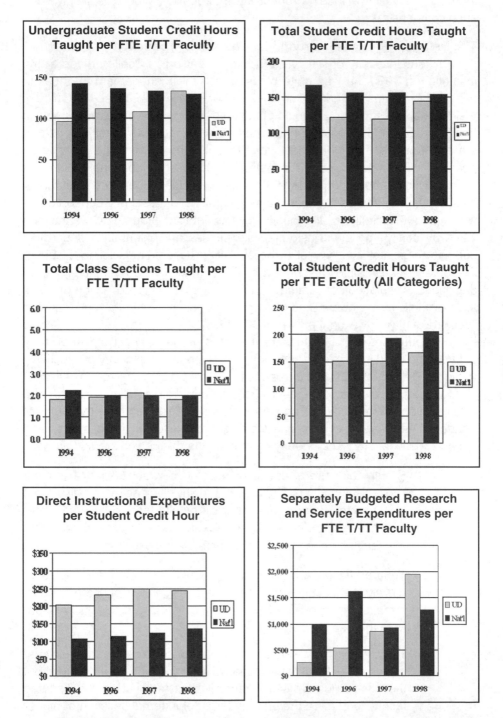

education. It is only sensible to have appropriate quantitative information to respond to those critics.

Provosts are busy people. In communicating productivity data to Provosts, it is important to capture their attention quickly. The Office of Institutional Research and Planning focuses on six productivity indicators from the Delaware Study, when communicating productivity data to the Provost:

- The number of lower division student credit hours taught per FTE tenured and tenure track faculty

- The number of undergraduate student credit hours taught per FTE tenured and tenure track faculty

- The number of organized class sections taught per FTE tenured and tenure track faculty

- The number of student credit hours taught by per FTE faculty, all categories of faculty combined

- The direct instructional cost per student credit hour taught

- The direct research/service expenditures per FTE tenured and tenure track faculty

In communicating these data, a picture is worth a thousand words. Displaying the data in spreadsheets are often most effective.

The Provost is provided with a summary sheet for each academic department at the University, focusing on the six Delaware Study variables identified earlier (Figure 1). This is a quick, pictorial snapshot of faculty productivity and instructional costs that enables the Provost to engage in constructive conversation with deans and department chairs as to why University of Delaware measures are similar to or different from the national benchmarks. Comparable national benchmarks are available for all four-year Carnegie institution types, as well as for the highest degree offered in a department. (It makes little sense to compare cost and productivity measures for an exclusively baccalaureate department with those of a program in the same discipline that offers extensive graduate instruction.)

In addition, the Delaware Study can provide the University, and its participants, with an analysis specific to a designated peer cohort. The peer analysis provides a set of peer norms, in addition to overall institutional ratios. The analysis focuses on individual institutional ratios for student credit hours and organized class sections according to course level and faculty type, faculty workload, and direct expenditures for instructional costs per student credit hour

45

and FTE student. It has been noted numerous times that departments at the University, as well as participating institutions in the Delaware Study, utilize the data provided by the peer analysis as a valuable resource to guide decision makers during discussions that focus on the following issues: accountability, competitiveness, marketing, and strategic planning. One of the greatest benefits of the Delaware Study is the peer analysis and the study's ability to provide decision makers with information to assess an institution's strategic position in relation to its peers.

A basic set of principles is adhered to when looking at either Budget Support Data or Delaware Study Data. No department is punished or rewarded based upon a single year of data. Any of a number of circumstances can produce spikes and troughs in the data. For example, faculty on sabbatical continue to be an instructional expenditure at a time when they are not teaching. Consequently, data are viewed over time to identify trends. Even then, the data are used as tools of inquiry to frame questions regarding why University of Delaware measures differ from national benchmark data. Because the Delaware Study is largely quantitative, it does not speak directly to quality issues that may well impact workload and cost measures (i.e., intentionally small class sizes, state-of-the art equipment, etc.). The benchmarking activity, nonetheless, allows departments to compare themselves with an external context.

Returning to the graphs in Figure 1, it is clear that the Provost's discussions have had an impact and have helped this department clarify its position relative to the national benchmark for research universities. Absent are any verifiable quality issues that would account for the disparity between the University of Delaware score and the benchmark. It was incumbent upon this department to take steps to move toward the benchmark and increase productivity. Undergraduate and total student credit hours taught by tenured and tenure track faculty, as well as separately budgeted research and service expenditures for that faculty group, have clearly converged with the national mean over the four years depicted in the graphs. The cost per credit hour taught is higher at the University of Delaware; however, that is not particularly troubling because the national benchmarks have not been adjusted to reflect the cost of living in the Philadelphia/Delaware region. The Washington D.C. to Boston corridor on the east coast, in which Delaware is located, is among the highest cost of living regions in the country. To attract and retain the best and brightest scholars, salaries have to be competitive with other institutions in the region; those salaries are significantly higher than national averages for faculty, by academic disciplines. Consequently, knowing that instructional costs are largely driven by faculty salaries, the direct instructional expenditure graph correctly depicts the competitiveness of University of Delaware's compensation policy.

Closing Thoughts

Faculty productivity is among the more sensitive topics of discussion in higher education today. This chapter has argued for a shift in the focus of faculty productivity analysis from inputs (i.e., "percentage of time spent on X") to outputs (i.e., "the products of faculty activity"). Once that transition is made, and links are established with the institutional budgeting process to reward productivity, controversies of the sort that occurred last year at Boston University should be significantly reduced, if not nonexistent.

References

America's Best Colleges, (1996, September 19). U.S. News and World Report. (pp. 91-105).

Joint Commission on Accountability Reporting. (1996) JCAR Technical Conventions Manual. Washington, D.C.: American Association of State Colleges and Universities.

Joint Commission on Accountability Reporting. (1997) JCAR Faculty Assignment Reporting. Washington, D.C.: American Association of State Colleges and Universities.

Middaugh, M. F. (2001) Understanding faculty productivity: Standards and benchmarks for colleges and universities. San Francisco, CA: Jossey-Bass Publishers.

National Association of College and University Business Officers. (1990) Financial accounting and reporting manual for higher education. Washington, D.C.: National Association of College and University Business Officers.

Rosovsky, H. (1992, September) From the belly of the whale. Pew Policy Perspectives. 4(3), (pp. A1-A8, B1-B4).

Schmidt, P. (1998, June 19) Governors want fundamental changes in colleges, question place of tenure. The Chronicle of Higher Education, (pp. A38).

U.S. Department of Education, National Center for Education Statistics. (1997) 1993 National Study of Postsecondary Faculty (NSOPF-93): Methodology Report. Washington, D.C.: Office of Educational Research and Improvement.

Wilson, R. (2001, February 2). It's 10 am: Do you know where your professors are? The Chronicle of Higher Education, (pp. A10-A12).

Zemsky, R. and Massy, W. (1999). Telling time: Comparing faculty instructional practices at three types of institutions. Change, 31(2), (pp. 55-58).

Zemsky, R. and Massy, W. (1990). Cost containment: Committing to a new economic reality. Change, 22(6), (pp. 16-22).

Chapter 4
Faculty Salary Analyses

Gerald W. McLaughlin, DePaul University
Richard D. Howard, Montana State University

In the case of tenured faculty, the Dean in principle allocates 45% of each year's salary increase in respect of scholarly productivity, 45% for teaching success, and 10% for professional service to Brown, the discipline and/or the community. These percentages are adjusted for untenured regular faculty members, who are actively discouraged by the administration from undertaking excessive service obligations, and lecturers and senior lectures, who by and large are expected to engage in professional development activities but not to do research. The Dean of the Faculty announced in the Fall of 1996 that one-third of the annual salary increment given for teaching success will henceforth also reflect the individual's service as an academic advisor. (Brown University, 1996 Self Study, Standard Five, 1996)

Introduction

Maintaining an appropriate faculty salary structure is one of the most important issues faced by college and university administrators and faculty. On most campuses, faculty salaries are a major component of institutional expenditures. The level of these expenditures reflects the fact that faculty are the primary input to the core functions of our institutions — learning, service, and research/scholarship.

Faculty salary analyses are a natural, important place to apply the skills, abilities, and knowledge housed in a typical institutional research function. As implied in Brown University's statement above, creating an appropriate salary structure is complex. It is both analytical and political in nature, requiring the use of quantitative and qualitative skills and methodologies to be applied within the context of the institution, its various disciplines, and the individual departments. The appropriate methodology for studying an institution's salaries must be selected, after considering the following issues in your situation:

1. Who is concerned about what? Why is it a concern? When does the analysis need to be completed?

2. Will the analysis involve measuring key components of the faculty role, such as advising, professional development, research, and "teaching success"?

3. How will these measures, reflecting these faculty attributes, be put into a quantitative perspective to support conclusions and decision making?

In this chapter, three aspects of faculty salary management are discussed. First, the uses of salaries by the institution are considered; second, data and analysis issues for conducting institutional faculty salary studies are presented (*equity, competitiveness, compression,* and *comparability*); and, third, a sequential set of steps for conducting a successful faculty salary analysis are outlined. (Note that many of the same issues that are related to and have an impact on faculty salaries exist for professional administrative staff, but will not be addressed in this chapter. The interested reader is referred to Toutkoushian, R. K. (2000), and Brozovsky and McLaughlin (1994). In addition, for discussions about part-time faculty salary issues, see California Postsecondary Education Commission (2001)). Finally, recent trends in the conduct of salary analyses and management are discussed. In the development of this chapter, the intent was to address issues associated with the study of faculty salaries in such a way that complemented and enhanced earlier work done on these issues. Hence, not included in this chapter are illustrations regarding the presentations of the results of salary analyses. Instead, the reader is referred to Howard, Snyder, and McLaughlin (1992) and other references for this chapter where illustrations of various ways to present the results of the analyses are provided.

Uses of and Influences on Faculty Salaries

As noted by the University Senate Budget Committee at the University of Oregon (2000), the proper consideration of faculty salaries requires that one "frame the faculty compensation issue and provide quantitative data as a basis for informed discussion." This "framing" of faculty salary and compensation issues is required for both management purposes of the institution and to address perspectives of society, particularly at public colleges and universities.

Management Uses of Salaries

Faculty salaries represent a means by which institutions pursue numerous management and administrative agendas. Moore and Amey (1993) have concluded that most differences in faculty salaries occur for reasons that reflect goals or objectives of the institution as related to an individual or specific program at a given point-in-time. Furthermore, as becomes apparent in the following discussion of the manner in which institutions use salaries to facilitate their goals, some of the uses seem to be in direct conflict with each other.

Salaries can be used as a motivator. The belief is that faculty will work harder and produce more to receive more money. Based on numerous studies, the conclusion seems to be that, while money is not the only motivator for faculty, if faculty do not feel they are receiving an appropriate salary, they will be dissatisfied. Neumann (1978) found that faculty rewards (compensation, recognition, and promotion) were clearly "the strongest predictor of faculty job satisfaction." (p 273) In addition, he found the strongest relationship was between rewards and pay satisfaction.

Salaries can be used to reward productivity. Faculty who are most productive would receive the largest amount of merit pay. Merit pay refers to granting salary increases based on the quality, or quantity, of the individual's performance. Difficulties in using merit pay practices often include the lack of an objective measure for the quality or quantity of performance that represents productivity. Frequently, there is also a failure to identify the characteristics of what is "meritorious." In other words, even when there is agreement that research grants represent productivity, there may be no agreement regarding which research grants are treated as more "meritorious" than others.

Closely connected to rewarding productivity is the use of salaries to reinforce the mission of the institution. If instruction is the most important component of the institution's mission, then it follows that good teachers should get higher salaries than good researchers. Anyone who has tried to translate a mission statement into objective outcomes is readily familiar with the pitfalls of trying to tie salary to institutional mission. An even bigger issue is that different activities seem to get different rewards in different disciplines. Smart and McLaughlin (1978) found that these differences vary in a significant manner, based on broad groups of disciplines. Their conclusion was that "any institution that attempted to develop a single institutional reward structure is likely to generate heated debates within the academic community for both philosophical and financial reasons." (p 53)

Some institutions may want to reward rank and seniority. This is consistent with the belief that, as the faculty member becomes more senior and professionally mature, he or she makes a greater contribution. It is also consistent with a belief that seniority alone is sufficient for higher pay. Rewarding rank and seniority is an issue since, at retirement, senior faculty who have been receiving raises while at the institution are often replaced by junior faculty who, while usually brought in at lower salaries, are often not brought in at sufficiently lower salaries when compared to remaining faculty. This results in salary compression for those remaining senior faculty. Even more prevalent is the fact that those conducting salary studies will typically find a statistically significant, negative quadratic term when modeling salary as a function of time-in-rank or time-at-the-institution, even when a linear form of salary is used, rather than the logarithm (Toutkoushian, 1998). This also means that variables like "time-in-rank" or "time-at-the-institution" may be found to be negatively related to faculty salaries. Haignere (2002) suggests computing a difference measure as the observed time for an individual minus the mean time and then using the square of the result to remove multicolinearity. She also discusses deriving measures such as subtracting year-of-hire from year-of-degree to form multiple time measures that are less correlated.

A salary structure may be established to reward different forms of productivity throughout the faculty member's career. In fact, faculty seem to be paid for doing different things as a function of their rank. Internal and external rewards change in importance during the career of the faculty member (Moore and Amey, 1993). In addition, the transition of the pay structure from one rank to another is not often smooth. In a study of some 12,000 ranked faculty members at research universities, the importance of institutional recognition (such as years-at-the-institution); duties (such as spending more time in administration and less in teaching); and, productivity (such as publications and funded research), changed in importance as predictors of salary for those in different ranks. For these faculty, pay structures existed that reinforced a shifting of their attention away from teaching and applied research toward publication and administration. Furthermore, the models that best explained these salaries were not simple extensions of a single model with different constants. The implication is that faculty at different ranks are expected to perform different functions (McLaughlin, Montgomery, and Mahan, 1979); as a result, different models (variables) are required to explain their salaries.

Recruitment and retention require the institution to be sensitive to the market value of a given faculty member and to subgroups of faculty in a given discipline with a given amount or type of experience. The continued shortage of qualified faculty in various disciplines, such as the engineering disciplines in the 1980's and the finance and accounting disciplines in the 1990's, meant that those entering with terminal degrees in these fields often received starting salaries that significantly compressed or sometimes exceeded (inversion) the more senior faculty salaries at the institution in the same discipline. The issue of salary compression became a concern in the late 1980's, when Blum (1989) documented that, during the 1980's, salary compression had become a prevalent problem on many campuses.

Society as a stakeholder and its influence

The institutional uses of salaries described above identify some of the issues and impacts an institution needs to consider in the development and management of an appropriate salary structure. The context in which these considerations must be debated reflects concerns about the rapidly increasing cost of higher education (*i.e.*, the tensions between providing a good *and* competitive wage to faculty versus higher education being an appropriately priced commodity). As noted earlier, faculty and staff salaries can frequently account for 70 to 80 percent of the operating expenses of an institution. Paulsen (2000) discusses the reason for swings in faculty salary growth when "faculty experienced a substantial loss of purchasing power due to salary increases well below the high rates of inflation in the 1970's, institutions made efforts to restore some of the lost purchasing power with salary increases that exceeded inflation rates in the 1980's." (p. 64) He further notes that this slowdown and catch-up process was not evenly distributed; furthermore, it attracted a great deal of unfavorable press. Generally, the institution needs to pay enough to give faculty a sufficient quality of life, while not paying excessive salaries and operating in an inefficient manner. The specific belief regarding salary is appropriate is usually group specific. The unevenness of the salary management process means that there are very likely many situations where individual faculty, or groups of faculty, have salaries substantially below what they should have or substantially higher than they should have.

Analyzing Salary Structures

What are the major concerns about faculty salary structures?
When the factors discussed above are implemented in a less than systematic and consistent process, various individuals and groups begin to raise concerns about the "fairness" of salaries. These concerns typically fall into one or more of the following groups of questions:

- Are salaries **equitable**? Do protected classes, such as women and minorities, earn salaries that are consistent with the majority?

- Are salaries **competitive?** Do faculty at your institution earn salaries consistent with discipline peers at other institutions?

- Are salaries **compressed**? Do salaries of new faculty approach or exceed salaries paid senior faculty in the same discipline?

- Are salaries **comparable**? When looked at in the context of your institution, across ranks and disciplines, and within the mission of your institution, do the salaries of various groups have the proper relationship to each other?

While the primary variables used in the analyses to answer these questions are often similar, traditional methodologies for addressing the questions differ. In fact, recommendations for dealing with one identified problem may result in the exacerbation of another. For example, dealing with competitiveness for junior faculty will almost certainly result in compression for senior faculty. While we present the analyses typically used to answer these questions as though they are stand alone activities, those conducting the analyses are cautioned to not move forward with either recommendations or actions to correct identified problems without considering the impact of these corrective actions on other aspects of the institution's salary structure.

Answering Questions about Faculty Salaries

As indicated above, four primary challenges to the integrity of faculty salaries and salary structures that need to be monitored by the institution are *equity, competitiveness, compression*, and *comparability*. In the remainder of this chapter, each challenge is presented with a description of the challenge, a discussion of some of the traditional analyses that are used to study the challenge, and the identification of, or the major issues in, the current status of the methodology used. In actual practice, the four challenges are not nearly as cleanly separated as the following discussion would suggest.

Equity: Do institution's salaries discriminate against protected groups?

This is always a big question, because the institution may be sued, and possibly fined, for violation of the laws that follow. In addition to being sued by an individual, an institution can be sued for an inappropriate salary structure by an entire group of individuals in a class action suit.

There seem to be three main legal positions describing basic protection under the law relating to salaries. Executive Order 11246, (2002) as amended, prohibits federal contractors and federally-assisted construction contractors and subcontractors, who do over $10,000 in government business in one year, from discriminating on the basis of race, color, religion, sex, or national origin.

In the Equal Pay Act of 1963, (2002) the plaintiff must prove:

1. Work was "equal" to that of employee of the opposite sex;
2. Work was performed at the same establishment; and,
3. Rate of pay of the plaintiff was less.

The burden then shifts to the employer to show pay difference is based on:

1. Seniority;
2. Merit system;
3. System that measures quantity or quality of production; and,
4. Some factor other than sex.

Title VII of the Civil Rights Act of 1964 (2002) prohibits employment discrimination including wage discrimination based on:

1. Race and Color;
2. National Origin;
3. Sex, Sexuality and Pregnancy; and,
4. Religion and Religious Practices.

This law applies to employers with 15 or more employees.

In addition to the three major anti-discrimination laws, the Age Discrimination in Employment Act of 1967 and the Older Workers Benefit Protection Act bar age based salary discrimination (Public Law 101-433) (2002). The Americans with Disabilities Act (ADA) of 1990 and Section 504 of the Vocational Rehabilitation Act of 1973 prohibits salary discrimination based on a disability. The Department of Justice (2002), provides a full discussion of the ADA at (http://www.usdoj.gov/crt/ada/adahom1.htm). On many campuses these rules are now becoming part of faculty handbooks (Calhoun Community College, 2001).

Many methods may be employed to judge the equity of the salaries of various groups. The simplest is a direct comparison, a t-test for two independent groups. This method is not used often because the t-test assumes the two groups are similar regarding the characteristics that determine salaries. Typically, the assumption is made in conducting salary equity studies that rational factors exist that cause or explain the individual salary differences. Modeling the salary structure to explain salary differences is typically accomplished by building an equation or a regression model. This statistical method is complex and easily biased. If you do not have a solid background in statistics, yet need to build a regression model, it is recommended that a statistical expert from your faculty or administration be included in the design and interpretation of the findings of the analysis. Always be aware, however, that regression only explains variation, it does not prove that various factors "caused" that variation.[1]

Two primary issues need to be addressed when using regression models to analyze salary equity: the metric for salary and the definition of fairness. The first issue deals with the metric form of salary as the dependent measure. Conceptually and mechanically the simplest method is to use a linear form of the salary. There are, however, strong and compelling conceptual reasons to use a logarithm transformation on the salary. This methodology, particularly favored by economists, is supported by the belief that the majority of salary raises are percentage increases and that faculty characteristics are related to the raise. In this case, larger salaries increase more rapidly than lower salaries. Conceptually, if the raises are based on a percentage, then any error will be a multiplicative error and can be assumed to be distributed in a log-normal distribution. The error then becomes normal after the logarithm is used and, therefore, the assumption of normal random errors is best met. In spite of this statistical consideration however, in general, one may well find that the use of a linear model of salaries does as well as using the logarithm of salaries. The advantage of using the linear model over the logarithm of the salary is that the complexity of interpreting, explaining, and making proposed adjustments is much more straightforward. However, the explanation of the linear regression results also can be extremely challenging in some situations. One of the difficulties associated with using a transformation of actual salaries, to log-salaries as the dependent variable in the regression model, is determining how well the alternative models fit the actual salary structure.

The second issue relates to defining fairness. Scott (1977) suggested that fairness should be defined from the *best white male* model. This position is also adopted by the AAUP sponsored update of Scott's work by Haignere (2002). A model predicting salaries is developed using the characteristics of white males; salary predictions are then made for the protected groups. (Scott, 1977, and Gray and Scott, 1980, Haignere, 2002) This methodology has some conceptual appeal in that if there is parity between the two groups, equations for one group *should be* appropriate for the other. However, problems arise: if white males do not make up the greatest proportion of the faculty, or if white males occupy a unique part of the salary structure and the relationship of salary to attributes is not linear. (Finkelstein, 1979, and McCabe, 1979)

An alternative methodology is to develop a regression model and determine whether the dummy variable "gender" makes a significant contribution to the explanation of salary. However, there are several problems with this approach.

It presupposes that the differences in salaries are attributable to a constant amount that is computed as the regression weight for gender. Thus, differences in a reward structure for men and women (where there are two equations) are masked.

Another issue involving the use of a single equation is related to the use of variables that are collinear. When the variables used to explain salary are related, or collinear, several problems can occur. Collinearity greatly decreases the stability of the equations, models, and interpretations. Several strategies to reduce the effects of collinearity include computing derived measures as mentioned earlier (Haignere, 2002), dropping one of the related variables, combining the related variables into a single variable, and using a statistical technique (such as ridge regression) to focus on key parts of the model. Collinearity also produces an inability to obtain a clear and unambiguous interpretation of the role of a specific variable in the explanation of the salary. This is a particular problem when the specific variable *is* the focus of the investigation, such as gender. The importance of contribution to variance explained accorded the variable (in this case gender), when it is included in a model with other variables, is related to the ability of the other variables to explain the variable of interest (gender). Stated another way, you cannot include gender in a regression equation and conclude that its regression weight accurately or appropriately reflects its ability to uniquely explain salary variability unless gender is statistically independent of all of the other independent variables. Otherwise, some of the difference in salaries would have been explained by other variables, were gender not in the equation.

One solution for determining the amount of salary that can be explained only by a specific variable, such as gender, is to use the following three-step procedure:

1. Develop a best model in the absence of the variable gender;

2. Calculate the residual, or unexplained, part of the salary for each individual; and,

3. Compare the residuals for those in various categories as defined by the variable of interest, *i.e.* males and females.

It should be noted that results of this procedure, or any regression procedure, do not prove that the variable of interest, in this case gender, caused the salary differences since such a proof requires the random assignment of faculty to categories (McLaughlin, Zirkes, and Mahan, 1983). It must also be recognized that the severity of multicollinearity will vary from institution-to-institution, from model-to-model, and may, or may not, be sufficient to cause concern (Moore, 1993).

In a similar procedure, Oaxaca (1973) noted that regression weights could be developed both from an equation developed for males *or* use regression weights from an equation developed for females. To look at "unexplained salary," one would use the means from the opposite group, with the regression weights from the first group. If one thought the males were paid fairly, then the use of the "male" model, with the means for the females, would help explain what it would be fair to pay the females. Newmark (1988) sought to remove this ambiguity. While the derivation is rather complex, Newmark proposes that one develop a single model without gender as described above. The mean difference between men and women on the independent variables would then be multiplied times the appropriate regression weight in the single model, in order to compute the explained part of salary difference. If this explained part of the salary is subtracted from the predicted total difference between the salaries, the remaining salary component is unexplained.[2]

As a result of the presence of collinearity, and the value of creating an unambiguous disaggregation of the salary difference, it is strongly recommended that gender not be used as a categorical measure in a regression model. If gender is not used as a categorical measure in a regression model, some form of the three-step procedure noted above, and the interpretation proposed by Newmark (1988), would seem to be most appropriate.

In addition to collinearity, the researcher must be aware that different salary structures could exist at the institution The most obvious differences will come from the fact that various professional activities are considered relevant in different disciplines (Smart and McLaughlin, 1978). There is also evidence that different activities are rewarded differently for different ranks (McLaughlin, Montgomery, and Mahan, 1979). Issues also exist regarding which variables are relevant, as well as which variables are free from "bias." For example, one of the more discussed variables is faculty rank. Relevance and bias are discussed more fully in a later section of this chapter as well as in the references provided. Obtaining a clear, objective statement regarding the relevance of characteristics and an agreement on the fairness of institutional recognitions, such as rank, are among the most important requirements of a good salary study, yet they are also among the most difficult of all steps.

Competitiveness: Can the institution attract and retain faculty?

The definition of competitiveness is much less technical than the definition of equity. In general, institutions want to pay their faculty a salary that ensures that they can obtain, maintain, and retain faculty possessing necessary ability, and of high enough quality, to support their programs and the institution's mission. Institutional needs of faculty will vary, depending on the level of degrees or certificates offered by the institution and the requisite requirements of regional and professional accreditation associations. Faculty qualities will also vary a great deal depending on the primary discipline focus of the institution, as well as where the institution intends to have excellence in programs. Finally, the quality of the faculty will vary by the level and breadth of skill desired on the part of the faculty at the institution. For instance, a university may prefer, but does not have to have senior faculty, rather than junior faculty, in some disciplines or as heads of some Centers or Institutes. Unfortunately, few of these characteristics are ever considered in the creation and maintenance of external databases.

One of the initial ways to study competitiveness is to examine salaries relative to their changes in purchasing power. If salaries at an institution do not keep pace with the local and regional economies, then the institution's faculty will be likely to go elsewhere (at least the quality faculty). Local price and cost of living indices should be used to monitor the relationship of faculty salary growth at the institution to rates of local or regional inflation.

Many countries have developed and published a price index and these are often available on the Web. For example, Switzerland (Swiss Statistics, 2002) has posted their price index at http://www.statistik.admin.ch/stat ch/ber05/eu0501.htm. Various regions within the United States have developed their own price indices. The price index for Seattle, Washington (2002) may be found at http://www.seattlechamber.com/infocenter/almanac costofliving.cfm. There is a caution however and if your institution is competing on a national basis for faculty, the adjustment of salaries for local costs may not be appropriate. In addition, a special Higher Education Price Index (HEPI) has been developed specifically to reflect the increasing costs of higher education. (Research Associates of Washington, 2001) If one assumes salaries should increase at the level of other education costs, the HEPI can be used to make salary adjustments.

External comparisons for a competitive position often include the salaries being paid by similar, or reference, institutions. Often, these institutions are referred to as peers; and the process is referred to as benchmarking. For an institution, the major issues behind this type of analysis are who to include in the reference group, and which standard to use as a statistic of the reference group. It should be noted that *peer* and *reference group* need to be thought of as possibly separate categories of institutions. (Teeter and Brinkman, 1992) The more appropriate term for a group used for external comparison is *reference group*; although, it is traditional to call this group "peers." Often these institutions are chosen for political, geographic, or other reasons and are, in fact, not institutional peers. Once the comparison group is chosen, then a decision must be made concerning what comparison statistic, reflecting the salaries for the reference group, should be used. Should the mean, the median, or a percentile be used? Over time, medians and percentiles tend to be more stable than means. When using a percentile as the comparative statistic, there is also the technical question of whether to use the actual percentile found in the reference group or instead, an estimate based on the standard deviation and assumptions of a normal distribution. While these sound like rather esoteric statistical issues, they may make a substantial difference in the salaries that you calculate as required for your institution to be competitive.

When analyzing the competitiveness of your institution's salary structure, it is necessary to have access to the salaries of your reference group. In some cases, data exchanges between similar institutions have been developed and the institutions within the exchange share these data. The Institutional Research Office at Oklahoma State University (OSU) annually collects average salaries by rank within discipline and region for most participating Land Grant Universities and many other major public institutions. The College and University Personnel Association (CUPA) annually collects salary and other demographic data about compensation for all institutions. If desired, you can request a data set that reflects the mean salaries for a specified reference group by discipline and rank. These discipline-rank means can then be weighted based on the proportion of faculty in various discipline-rank combinations at your institution to give an estimate of what the salaries would be if the reference group had your institution's mix of faculty. Using data from these sources, it is also possible to conduct analyses that examine the competitiveness of specific disciplines or groups of disciplines. Another important measure of competitiveness is the relative standing of salaries of beginning assistant professors. These data also are available in both the CUPA and the OSU data exchanges. You do need to be careful to ensure that the faculty categories of interest are sufficiently broad so as to have reasonable stability in the reference group and at your institution. A minimum of 10 to 20 faculty members for each reported average is recommended.

In addition, salaries and compensation are provided in Academe (2001). These data are comparable to the NCES/IPEDS annual data collection, so they do not have the discipline level data that are contained in the OSU/CUPA data. The advantages of the Academe/NCES data are that they include institutional identification, information about the cost per type of benefit, and mean salary information by region and type of institution.

These sources of data are starting points in establishing your institution's competitive position in the marketplace. Collecting information on the offers made to faculty that were accepted and declined will enhance your understanding of the competitiveness of your institution. Some of these offers will be counteroffers made to retain continuing faculty, as well as offers to new faculty. Collect as much information as possible about the offers made by reference institutions. It is important to remember that not all "perks" are included in the salary. Teaching load agreements, research facilities, location, and travel funds are only a few of the items that may accompany salary offers that faculty receive. These, in addition to salaries and benefits, combine to define the competitiveness of your institution to attract and retain faculty.

Competitive analyses are normally done by comparing averages of the salaries at your institution to the average salaries at some external reference institution or group of institutions. This can be done at the rank level, at the discipline level, and/or at the institutional level. Another option is to compute ratios of the institution's mean salaries to the mean salaries of the reference group, then compare these ratios to a standard such as 1.00 to identify the amount of relative competitiveness. The use of indices and adjustments, however, increases the complexity of interpretation and the difficulty of the explanation.

Compression: Have internal salary adjustment practices or recent hires compressed or inverted salaries?

Defined at the University of Oregon (2000) as "the erosion of compensation as a factor distinguishing faculty ranks," compression appears when the difference in salaries based on rank, and/or seniority, is less than desired. This is frequently considered as being the relationship between the average salary of those in one rank and the average salary of those in an adjacent rank. Compression can also be viewed as a function of the average salaries of faculty based on their years-in-rank or their years-at-the-institution.

As part of seniority, it is possible to look at compression as a function of starting assistant professor salaries, as related to the salaries of assistant professors with three to five years experience. In some institutions, such as Indiana State University (ISU) (2000), faculty senates have resolved that compression is "a first priority and that faculty salary 'compression' adjustments account for the number of years at ISU, number of years-in-rank at ISU, number of promotions, and number of 'merit' or other high performance recommendations at ISU (so as not to 'cancel out' performance achievements)."

Discipline and institutional policy are important factors in defining compression. For example, it is likely that many faculty on part-time appointments would not be considered in the various definitions of compression, because they are often seen as being hired to do a specific task where seniority is not a basis for additional pay. There is a need to ensure that issues of compression are not confounded with legal equity questions, in which faculty with more seniority establish that their lower pay is based on some illegal discrimination. It also may be important to account for terminal degrees and certifications, where appropriate. For example, while senior faculty may have lower average pay, the situation may be a function of superior qualifications of the junior faculty rather than simple compression.

A simple method for analyzing salary compression is to compute the ratios of salaries paid to junior faculty compared to those paid to senior faculty. This is the method used by the Office of Planning and Budget for the University System of Missouri (1999). In this case, the mean salary is computed for each rank; the difference in mean rank salaries is then examined over time and across different institutions. The relationship between averages is viewed as an algebraic difference, as well as a ratio difference. After the resulting ratios were graphed, it was determined that while compression had become a visible problem in the mid-1980's to the mid-1990's, the situation was improving and by 1999 had reached the same level of salary spread as in the 1970's.

This illustrates one of the challenges in looking at salary compression. Certainly, average salaries of senior faculty should typically be greater than the average salaries of faculty in junior ranks. However, how much larger salaries of senior faculty should be in order to reflect an uncompressed salary structure is not self-evident. The Missouri study implied that the salary structure was in good shape in the 1970's. When the ratios are comparable to what they were in the 1970's, it is assumed that salaries are in balance. Another methodology involves comparing the ratios of average salaries by rank, from a reference group of institutions to those at your institution. When the ratios at your institution are at the same level as those in the reference group, it can be concluded that salaries are comparably spread. At the institutional level, it may be necessary to extend the analysis to the discipline level, comparing levels of compression across various disciplines. In conducting this type of cross-disciplinary comparisons, the following questions will need to be answered: *Do some disciplines have more of a compression problem than others?* and *How do the differences in compression among disciplines at your institution compare to those found in the reference group?*

A second way to look at compression is to compute the average salaries for faculty in rank, based on time-in-rank. This approach is particularly appropriate when the intent of your institution is to pay higher salaries to the more senior faculty in each rank. Since there should normally be 10 to 20 faculty members in a category in order to give the average salaries appropriate stability, groupings for years-in-rank need to be developed. While the grouping strategy depends on the number of faculty, which in turn, depends on the number of different disciplines grouped together, categories such as 0-1 years, 2-4 years, 5-7 years, 8-11 years, etc. are usually good guidelines. In this type of analysis, the averages for assistant professors with more than seven years in rank may show decreasing average salaries; this may be seen as consistent with the mission of the institution as these faculty are not producing per promotion and tenure criteria of the institution.

A third way to look at compression, particularly in a case where the sample for time-in-rank categories is rather small, is to develop a regression model, as in the equity process, leaving out the various measures of time-in-rank (and probably years-at-institution). The residual compared to time-in-rank for those in the various ranks should probably show an increasing positive salary residual, when associated with the increasing time-in-rank. You need to be aware that decreases in salary cannot be solely, or significantly, attributed to age. For additional perspective on age discrimination suits, the reader may wish to follow the SUNY case in which an age discrimination class action suit for more than 10,000 faculty over the age of 40 has been filed. (Ourworld, Compuserve, 2002) Also, for a more complete discussion of the issues of compression analyses, see Snyder, McLaughlin, and Montgomery (1992).

Comparability: Is the salary structure consistent with institutional purpose and intent?

As noted at the first of this chapter, the concern for the appropriateness of salaries typically involves issues of equity, compression, and competitiveness. (Brown, 1996) When these factors are combined and, as at Brown, placed in the context of the institution, then the institution is moving toward comparable faculty salaries. In other words, the institution is developing a salary structure that will be internally and externally consistent and is more likely to be accepted by the majority of the faculty as being basically fair. This characteristic called Comparability is the fourth criterion of a well managed salary structure. Comparability combines the other three criteria and views them within the context of the institution and its environment.

Comparability must be considered when the institution reviews the salaries of various groups of faculty relative to the salaries of other groups of faculty. Comparability primarily combines the assessment of equity, compression, and competitiveness within the context of the institutional mission and the concern of fairness in terms of professional maturity and institutional seniority. The example of the policy from Brown University's self study is an excellent example of how the various elements of salary were tied together as the institution sought to achieve comparability within their salary structure.

In terms of an analytical procedure, the question becomes how best to put salaries into the broader context of the institution. There does not seem to be a traditional methodology for this analysis, as much of the prior research on salaries has looked at the separate salary issues discussed above. While each type of analysis has the advantage of looking at a specific problem, much of the audience, as well as many of the stakeholders, will be looking at a combination of the issues simultaneously. Comparability is particularly dependent on an objective discussion of why faculty are to be rewarded, as discussed earlier, and what the appropriate elements should be that drive the salary structure at the institution.

One approach in determining comparability is to build a regression model to predict salaries using appropriate measures, then analyzing the residuals in relation to specific categories of faculty. This analysis is an extension of the Braskamp and Johnson model (1978) in which they identified variables in terms of their "rational" nature. For example, suppose the average residuals for the faculty in the College of Commerce were being compared to the average residuals in the College of Engineering. The comparison needs to then be interpreted in terms of the institution's mission and priorities. If the colleges share an equal importance in the mission of the institution, the average residuals should be about equal. One should also look at average residuals based on seniority measures. If years-in-rank is included in the model, the average residual for those with only a few years of service should be about the same as the residual for those with a large number of years of service. At a research university, the average residual for departments with large amounts of research should be more positive than the average residual for departments with lower amounts of research. The intent is to explore, describe, and explain the status of the salary structure within the context of the institution.

Steps in Conducting a Faculty Salary Analysis

The preceding discussion focused on analyses addressing issues that challenge the integrity of an institution's faculty salary structure. In conducting faculty salary analyses, it has been found that there exists a sequence of steps that tend to make a salary analysis more useful and less painful. This sequence is described in the following section. It should be noted that, while these steps are presented as occurring in a general sequence, they tend to overlap in practice. On occasion, the researcher will need to return to an earlier step (*i.e.*, when the results of analyses vary widely from expectations). In addition, these steps are presented with the explicit intent that they be considered guidelines that will need to be modified with respect to your institution's situation. Finally, the study provides an analysis of the institution's salary structure at a particular point-in-time. Interpretation of the results of the analysis will usually lead to the development of strategies to address problems that have been identified. It is important to develop and implement a monitoring process to assess the impact of the strategies that have been implemented (Hosler, 1996; Haignere, 2002).

The steps presented in the following section reflect a sequential set of five activities proposed in an earlier work for the creation of useful decision support information (McLaughlin, Howard, Balkan, and Blythe, 1998). This set of activities provides a structure for conducting a salary analysis that reflects the issues that have to be addressed, in order to conduct a successful salary study. The activities also build on an earlier work salary analysis (Howard, Snyder, and McLaughlin, 1992).

1) Conceptual Model and Measures

The first step in most salary analyses is to develop a conceptual model of what variables or measures should explain faculty salaries (McLaughlin, Frost and Schultz, 1995). The model shown in Figure 1 may be used as a starting point. You must ask the question: For what activities and services does the institution pay faculty? The following is a brief discussion of the components of this model.

Entities: The three primary entities in this model are the individual, the institution, and the discipline. The *individual* has a set of personal characteristics, abilities, motivations, and experiences. The *institution* has a purpose and a set of resources to pursue that purpose. The *discipline* has standards for professional competence and a paradigm for examining the faculty role and level of competence.

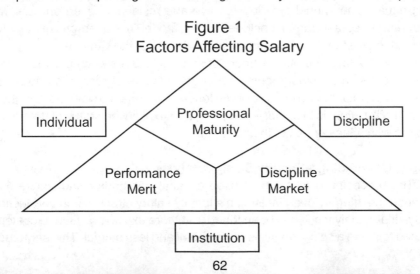

Figure 1
Factors Affecting Salary

Attributes: The entities interact with three primary attributes: merit, professional maturity, and market. *Merit* reflects the quality and quantity of work that the faculty member produces. It is considered within the context of the institution; faculty activity should be relevant to the intent or purpose of the institution in order for there to be value in the activity. *Professional maturity* includes years of service to the institutional and to the profession. This maturity often results in shifting the faculty's responsibilities and roles over time. *Market* is the supply of faculty and the demand for their services. Breneman and Youn (1988) have identified both internal and external markets. Internal labor markets operate within an organization, individual campus, university system, or educational union. They value key disciplines, stable employment, and promotional hierarchies. External labor markets involve the industry and tend to price and allocate labor on the basis of economic relationships, such as competition. There are three primary components around which external labor markets form: teaching, research, and extension. Additional factors, such as institutional size, location, and racial/ethnic diversity influence the formation of sub-markets.

The development of the theoretical, or conceptual, model has to be built with an understanding of who the key stakeholders are and what their involvement is in the process. Often the process of defining the model has started before the institutional research function becomes involved. Typically, a question arises about the fairness of salaries by various groups seeking to exert leverage over the salary structure. Invariably, a problem or potential problem has been identified, and key forces in the institution have decided that something needs to be done to address the issue. The first part of salary analysis, for the typical situation, is heavily dependent on Terenzini's (1993) contextual knowledge to define and delimit the situation. In almost all cases, the senior administrative or academic officer - a provost or vice president of academic affairs, or dean of instruction - is involved by virtue of having managed the current "traditional processes" of determining salaries. Typically, there is at least one opposition group who feels they are not getting a fair salary. Often, there are secondary groups who are looking for some relief from situations they do not consider fair. Sometimes the terrain includes lawyers; sometimes the lawyers are working on an active or a proposed lawsuit (McKee, 1997). The institutional research function often needs to start with an articulation of the problems and an identification of the goals of the salary analysis. The ability to involve these various groups in a collaborative effort will depend on the specific situation, but the concerns of all involved must be identified and stabilized.

If the issue involves an individual, or a small group of individuals, then the analyses may be fairly direct. For example an individual salary may be compared to the salaries of those in a select group. The focused group may be internal, such as other faculty at the same rank in the department. In other cases, the analysis may be external, such as using the average salary and raises of a reference group in the same rank and discipline. Even in these limited situations, it may be better to include a broader analysis that includes a wide range of faculty. The following includes a discussion of the analyses that are institution-wide, such as class action concerns for gender and minority salaries.

One of the first decisions in designing the study is to determine whose salaries are to be included in the study. Typically, it must be decided whether or not include part-time faculty, of those not in the tenure-track process, those not in traditional functions of instruction and scholarly work (such as extension, library, and externally funded research faculty), and those not in one of the three professorate ranks. Most traditional studies restrict their investigation to a definition of full-time tenure-track assistant to full professors engaged primarily in instruction, a definition similar to that used in the IPEDS/AAUP data. The desire to be inclusive of various types of personnel such as non-tenure track instructors, research faculty, librarians, etc. must be balanced against the reality of the situation. If the study includes subgroups that are being paid for different abilities and efforts, it is very likely that multiple models will need to be included in the analysis of the structure. For example, term appointed instructors might be paid a flat rate across the college based on their years of teaching while tenure-track faculty may be paid based on their discipline. If you wanted to fit one model to the combination of the subgroups you would need to moderate the regression of the independent measures of time and discipline based on subgroup membership.

A second step in this phase of the analysis is to select measures about individual faculty and general institutional or discipline measures. These measures traditionally include demographic characteristics within the institution, professional maturity, professional activity, and market factors. The following question must be addressed at this point: *For what activities and services is this group being paid for?* See Braskamp and Johnson (1978) for a detailed discussion of the rationality of using various factors or measures for examining salaries.

The next step is to determine a methodology for looking at the primary concern. If the concern is equity, then comparisons must be made between various subgroups defined by gender and/or by ethnicity and/or by age. If the concern is compression or competitiveness, then other methodologies previously described must be used. A final step in the design phase is to determine what function the results of the study will serve. These discussions must result in an acceptable level of concurrence, if not a consensus, among the stakeholders, if the salary study is to be successful.

2) Obtain Data and Make it Usable

Once a conceptual model and measures have been identified, the second step is to obtain and validate a database. The specific elements need to be collected and checked. If a measure is important and is not maintained in institutional databases, then the data must be collected. This frequently occurs with measures such as date-of-first employment, where the data are typically stored in a payroll history database and not a personnel database. The data should be audited to make sure they are complete, allowable, consistent, and feasible. Complete means the data are there and are accessible. Allowable means that the attribute is an authorized value for the data element. Consistent means that combinations of data are interpretable. Feasible means that the data should be logical. If it appears that half of the faculty at your institution have degrees from an institution that is not readily recognizable then there is most likely a problem in the data definitions of the file you working with.

The collection and correction of data requires that someone be available that is knowledgeable of the faculty and their individual situations. The researcher should be particularly sensitive to strange events occurring with the salary, such as the inclusion of supplemental pay for distinguished faculty; payment in non-financial components, such as "free housing"; faculty in partial retirement working for partial pay; prior experience in senior administrative positions; and, other unique situations too numerous to mention. The researcher should be aware that just because the system has a element referred to as *starting date*, does not mean that the data are available, accurate, or consistently collected and coded.

Specific variables selected for inclusion in a salary analysis must meet several criteria. The variables need to be relevant to market, maturity, and merit. The variables need to have sufficient reliability and be current enough to reflect recent salary adjustments and changes in faculty status. The data also need to be available and accessible with a reasonable amount of effort. The terms "sufficient," "adequately," and "reasonable" are defined within the context of the institution and the situation that precipitated the study or process. These data can come both from external and internal sources.

In terms of external data, work in salary analyses has developed on several fronts. First, the presence of external data for salaries has become more refined, as discussed in the previous section on competitiveness. You should consider identifying a group of "peer," or reference, institutions, evaluating average salaries for your institution, at the discipline and rank level, to the averages at the reference institutions. In one case, the uses of these data sources resulted in the following concern: "Resources need to be reallocated in order to progress toward rectifying exploitive exempt staff salaries at LCSC. Our salary benchmark should be raised higher than median CUPA comparison data (to 60th percentile in $, at minimum)" (Lewis and Clark State College, 2001).

In terms of internal data, there are many potential variables to include in a salary model. McLaughlin, Smart, and Montgomery (1978) studied the direct, indirect, and total influence of 39 variables associated with salary. More recent studies, which included multiple institutions, have used a large number of measures obtained from NCES/National Survey of Postsecondary Faculty (NSOPF) studies of faculty in 1988 and 1993. These data include institutional characteristics, faculty characteristics, and faculty activities in terms of time spent and outcomes such as publications and grants (Toutkoushian, 1994b, 1998).

Studies at individual institutions tend to be much less likely to have such extensive databases. In fact, as previously mentioned, most institutional personnel systems have evolved from payroll systems that also have some career history of promotion and tenure. In most of the institutional level studies, discipline and rank are found to be the major determinates of salary. Rank and discipline are often used in regression analysis as moderator variables or as dummy variables. The tradeoff is that, if used as moderator variables, the groups may become too small for valid results. The problem with always using these measures as dummy variables is that different disciplines tend to have different reward structures (McLaughlin, Montgomery, and Mahan, 1979, Smart and McLaughlin, 1978). This is the same type of issue as encountered when you group unlike types of personnel together and fit one regression line, with or without the categorical measure. Decisions regarding the grouping of faculty to look at the issues of different salary structures should be geared toward having a sufficiently large group with sufficient homogeneity. Braskamp and Johnson (1978) discuss using discipline categories, in addition to the discipline-based average salaries. For the purpose of their analysis additional discipline categorical measures and non-rational internal measures are considered. [3]

Differences in average faculty salaries between disciplines are often considerable in both internal and external comparisons. In a survey of 18 disciplines in large, mostly public institutions, Hamermesh (1988) found a $25,000 difference between full professors in law and full professors in fine arts. The CUPA and OSU data sets previously mentioned provide excellent external data for conducting these types of comparisons.

In addition to major differences in salaries attributed to discipline, there are traditionally large differences in salaries associated with rank. While rank is essential for most competitiveness, compression, and comparative analyses, there has been a great deal of discussion about the appropriateness of using rank as a measure in studies of salary equity. In her work on performing salary equity analyses, Scott (1977) suggested that rank not be included as one of the variables in the analysis, because the system that was suspect of discrimination in salary was the same system that was responsible for many of the rank decisions. For instance, frequently women do tend to have lower ranks than men (Toutkoushian, 1999).

The concern and debate regarding using rank in salary equity analyses continues with Becker and Toutkoushian (1999). They summarize 24 studies, in which the majority did not use rank (six), presented results with and without rank in the model (nine), or tested for gender bias in the current ranks (six). Only three studies used rank without further consideration. The issues involved in the decision to include rank in salary analyses are summarized by Boudreau, et. al. (1997). There are several strategies for conducting a salary study. One strategy is to run the models with and without rank, then interpret the difference (as done in Boudreau et. al., 1997). However, the researcher then risks having two different conclusions. There is also a problem with specification bias, because of the omission of a factor (rank) that does have a major relationship to salary.

Another alternative is to use the part of rank that does not seem to be contaminated by, or related to gender (Becker and Toutkoushian, 1999). This, while conceptually strong, is statistically rather complicated. Another choice is to determine if rank is biased; and, if so you should avoid using it as a measure. Other choices include determining if the current rank seems to be biased by looking at proportions at the various ranks (Haignere, 2002), explaining it with a linear model (Toutkoushian, 2000) or determining if the process that produced the rank seems to be biased with an analysis such as a Log-Linear analysis (Hinkle, Austin, and McLaughlin, 1989). Haignere (2002) concludes that one should test rank for bias and then use it in the analysis. If it is biased, then she would conclude that the estimate of descrimination shown in the model is conservative because if more women had been promoted, their salaries would be even more depressed for the higher rank than for their current rank.

Time variables such as time-in-rank, time-at-institution, and time-since-degree, are very helpful. If compression is being studied, it is helpful to look at the average salaries based on such variables, identifying the specific variables as the one most associated with that for which your institution intends to pay more. These measures tend to be highly correlated. When used in regression analyses, they will usually result in manifesting collinearity problems. In addition, they seem to have non-linear relationships with salaries; therefore, the usefulness of quadratic terms should be determined, particularly when modeling the logarithm of salary.

When the number of local promotions is used in regression models, which specify salary as the dependent variable, there is some evidence that the quadratic form of time-since-degree and time-at-institution ceases to be statistically significant in explaining salary. This comes from the finding that at these institutions, the more local promotions, the greater the disadvantage to faculty in terms of salary growth

Another factor determining salary differences at some institutions is the level of degree held. Because the Ph.D. is not the terminal degree in disciplines such as dance and theatre, this variable must be used with caution. Other possible measures that might influence salary include tenure status, distinguished status (such as University Distinguished Professor), campus location (if multiple campuses exist), administrative responsibilities, and type of appointment (academic year versus calendar year) to name a few. Faculty activity may also influence salary. There is evidence that time spent on various types of activities is rewarded differentially, depending on the academic discipline. In some institutions, differences in salary may increase depending on how much a faculty member teaches. However, this relationship may be the inverse at some research institutions where teaching is related to lower salaries. Yuker (1984) gives a comprehensive description of some of the alternatives and complexities of measuring faculty effort. Recent work has also looked at citations, (Toutkoushian, 1994a, 1994b), publications (Toutkoushian, 1998), and special recognitions for sustained eminence (Boudreau, et. al., 1997). The philosophical and conceptual issue becomes deciding how your institution rewards (or wants to reward) various types of effort and the quality of that effort. The empirical issue is the degree to which you can develop appropriate measures for these variables.

3) Analyze Data to Create Information

Performing the analysis is not typically a single bold surgical run of the data through a standard computer program. Often the analysis is an iterative and, hopefully, converging and heuristic series of events that typically ends when the lack of time and the adequacy of results converge in the presence of the key decision makers. In any analysis, there needs to be a methodology driven by the conceptual model; the intended use of the results which is also relevant in developing the conceptual model; and, the adequacy of the data which may or may not have been fully understood when the process started. Also, as results begin to emerge, there may be a shifting of the study design and of the collection of additional data. In research, if this is done on purpose, the approach is sometimes referred to as a grounded theory and the entire process can be described as a meta-analysis with nested studies. More often than not, the methodology will be less than linear and logical. Change should be anticipated and greeted with incremental opportunism. In addition, the researcher must set a "drop-dead" date at which the analysis must end for the project to be successful.

The specific analyses will involve comparisons, which most likely will be some type of adjusted comparisons. Competition analyses involve the comparing of salaries to external reference groups. Compression analyses compare average salaries of adjacent ranks of faculty, sometimes adjusting for time-in-rank. Equity analyses compare gender or ethnicity of faculty, often adjusting for demographic characteristics, market, and professional maturity. Comparability analyses looks at internal and external consistency, adjusting for or at least considering all measurable factors that the institution says are important in determining salary.

As noted previously, the analytic tools range in complexity from simple ratios and chi-square analyses to two-stage non-linear regression and Hieratical Equation Modeling. Every analysis decision has statistical and political implications. For example, the inclusion of variables such as the number of local promotions, rank, and discipline are political, as well as statistical decisions. You should be aware that most groups of stakeholders know these political and statistical issues well.

4) Deliver the Information and Facilitate Understanding

After the analysis phase has been completed, including often iteration back to data collection or even back to the process definition phase, it is time to deliver the results and report the findings. This delivery of results is one of the most important phases of the project. If the analysis was conducted to investigate a legal situation, then delivering and reporting the results will typically be very proscribed by the legal situation. You may be conducting the analysis for a lawyer, in which case the results would be reported to the lawyer. In cases where a legal issue is not the primary driving force behind the analysis, then the strategy for the delivery of results should be coordinated with key stakeholders. Typically, this includes the senior academic officer, again the institutional lawyer, and sometimes representatives of the key stakeholders identified in the definition and development phase of the project. When the analysis results in the development of an expected salary and the computation of the difference between the expected salary versus the actual salary is a factor of the analysis, a key issue becomes the amount of individual identification that should be reported with the expected and residual salary. Most likely these results with be treated with the confidentiality of personnel merit ratings.

The aggregate results may be presented to a working group or groups who discuss the results, then conclude if problems exist and where they exist. You may then be asked to do additional analyses. Once the use of group processes has been completed, if appropriate, individual faculty statistics should be provided to an appointed person in the management process. If you work in a public institution in a state that has freedom of information laws, some of the results will have to be shared with the media. It is likely that statistics about individual faculty will be restricted as sensitive because, at least partially, they represent a combination of perceptions associated with individual merit decisions and starting salaries. In some situations, the senior academic officer may meet with deans to discuss individual cases.

In terms of the actual report, it is desirable to provide both tables and extensive figures reflecting the results. If an index or transformation on the salaries has been done, you should provide some of the results in terms of dollars. Detailed documentation of the methodology and analyses should accompany the report in an appendix. Know your audience. Communicate results and conclusions with them using both language and contexts consistent with their backgrounds and understanding of the issues.

5) Using the Results

Use of the results will come from conclusions reached by interpreting the results within the context of the situation. If there is a specific focus, it may be feasible to compute the amount of funds needed to rectify the situation. For example, if the issue is compression, a desired standard may be defined as the point where the ratio of rank averages at your institution is not more compressed than the ratio of rank averages found in the reference groups. In this case, you can take the actual average and the external average and compute the funds required to bring the average salaries into line (Snyder, McLaughlin, and Montgomery, 1991, and Snyder, Hyer, and McLaughlin, 1994). In cases involving equity concerns, computing the explained and unexplained part of the difference in residuals will provide a base for calculating the amount of money needed to make up unexplained differences (Newmark, 1988). The manner in which you estimate the size of the problem interacts with the procedure used to fix the problem. Questions of merit, equity, compression, competitiveness, and comparability may have to be addressed (Wenger and Girard, 2000).

There are five issues that will factor into implementation of the results of an analysis. First, there are numerous ways to adjust for lack of equity in salaries (Toutkoushian, 2000). These different methods have an effect on where the researcher begins to determine the deficit, as well as whether the researcher assumes the problem to be a problem for all members of the group or only for some individuals in the group. Second, often salary increases most likely will not result in the salary deficits going to zero, because the allocation of funds, particularly as part of a set of annual raises coupled with the changes in the faculty, will shift the model. This shift will probably result in a reduced, but still existing, disparity. This disparity is most likely when the amount of funds is limited. Third, in rectifying the salary inequities, particularly if part of the strategy to make the pay situation more appropriate for a selected subgroup of faculty, it is possible that you will uncover individuals that need a salary supplement, even if they were not included in one of the initial groups of concern. When looking at pay discrimination against women, it is not uncommon to identify men with salaries that are much lower than can be explained by current policies and to make some adjustments in their pay. Fourth, the demographics of the faculty may be such that correcting one problem may exasperate another. For example, if funds are allocated to women in junior ranks, compression will likely increase. If funds are allocated to senior faculty, competitiveness for entry-rank faculty will likely be reduced. Fifth, and finally, most likely funding will be inadequate to resolve the problems in one year. It is very likely that the study will need to be conducted on an annual basis to monitor the effectiveness of a multi-year strategy, or strategies, put in place to address the identified problem(s). As with many processes that deal with quality, improving a salary structure is a long-term journey not quickly rectified in one year (Hostler, 1996).

Recent Trends in Studying Salaries

The study of salaries has been an active topic of investigation for the past several decades. In early studies the appropriateness of using multiple techniques and models to examine salaries was discovered. These studies also produced a conceptual framework in which variables are identified that should be used, particularly when a linear model is employed. This body of knowledge has been extended through the publications of the Association for Institutional Research (AIR) and presentations at AIR Forums.

Recently, there have been three trends in the study of salaries. First, during the past decade there has been a great deal more data and information about salary studies available on the Internet. Second, faculty salaries have become a concern internationally. Third, salaries are now public information in many situations.

1) Internet Documents

In terms of the increase of available information, a search of the Internet using the search engine Google and the key search words "faculty salary compression equity competition" returned 455 sites in September, 2002. These sites include university senate white papers on policies related to salary (University of Oregon, 2000, Harrigan, 1999) and discussions on salary processes dealing with equity. The University of Wisconsin-Madison (2000) used a procedure for the 2000-2001 year involving input on specific cases from the deans, self-nomination, and department chairs. In this procedure, committees and various senior administrators reviewed recommendations and the results of proposed adjustments on the salary distributions. Staff assistance was provided from the university including legal and analytical support. Salary adjustments came from individual college budgets. The scheduled time for the process was nine months. Other guidance regarding salary studies is available from professional associations such as the Association of American Medical Colleges at http://www.aamc.org/members/wim/wimguide/start.htm. This Web site contains a statement on the role of women in medicine (Bickel, Croft, and Marshall, 1996), as well as an excellent discussion on conducting a salary equity study (Hostler, 1996). Potential purposes of a salary equity study, primary considerations (such as what needs to be decided before the study starts, what factors impact salary, and the role of leadership), and methodologies (such as comparisons, the role of disciplines and rank, and the use of regression) are discussed along with advantages and disadvantages of each.

You must remember to balance this increased availability of resources and discussions with a caution. Much of this new flow of information does not go through the quality control process of a refereed publication or a paper presented at a professional meeting. The Internet allows those who have opinions, and persistence, to make their perspectives available. The person who uses Internet-based information must have the methodological capacity, through their own knowledge or through the experience of colleagues, to sort appropriate methodologies from inappropriate methodologies and supported conclusions from perceived opinions.

2) Internationalization

The discussion of salary issues has become a topic of international concern. Included in the international forum is an articulation on broader issues of salary equity context in society and in higher education. The Women's Electoral Lobby Australia, Inc. (2002) provides access to the monograph *Gender Equity in Australian University Staffing* by Dr. Clare Burton (1998). Another example of the international interest in salary equity is the activity of the Status of Women Canada (2002) . There are also Internet sites that include links to numerous country sites such as the International Women's Site (2002).

3) Part-Time Faculty

The concern regarding salary equity has extended to part-time faculty. Researchers are now analyzing the comparability of part-time faculty salaries with those of the full-time faculty. These studies have been recorded in the faculty senate minutes at the University of Louisville (July 1999) as well as in the report to the California Postsecondary Education Commission, (2001). This interest has developed in reaction to the growing practice of using part-time faculty and faculty appointed for a fixed term for instructional purposes, particularly at research universities.

4) Freedom of Information

A third change in policy has been to make faculty salaries public information. For example, in Ontario, Canada, salaries for university employees who make more than one hundred thousand dollars annually are posted on the Internet in order to comply with the Ontario Public Sector Salary Disclosure Act of 1996 (2001). In Virginia, salaries of all faculty at public universities and colleges who make more than ten thousand dollars are part of public record based on the Freedom of Information Act. (http://legis.state.va.us/codecomm/valac/foiaview.htm)

Many of our institutions can no longer make salary a private conversation between the institution and individual employees. Any faculty member at a public institution can now judge the appropriateness (or fairness) of their salary for themselves. This free flow of information should improve the quality of salary data on our campuses and in public databases. It will also make it feasible, and much easier, for a wide range of individuals to analyze the data and draw their own conclusions. "Freedom of Information" also means that if you are conducting a salary study at a public institution, it is very likely that the results of your study and your methodology will be considered a matter of public record.

Summary

As is evident by the number of factors and issues discussed previously, the analysis and understanding of faculty salaries are complex and challenging processes. Concern over losing a lawsuit is real and can occur when age, race, gender, disabilities, and other protected characteristics become solely and significantly related to salary. More than being a possible reason for losing a lawsuit, however, salaries are instrumental in accomplishing the intent of the institution through governance and administration. Institutional researchers have made major methodological advances in the field of salary studies, working with economists, statisticians, and other professionals. However, there is still much to be accomplished and some work to be redone. Complicating the situation is the reality that the rules governing salary management are changing and new challenges are emerging. It is difficult to develop, implement, and maintain a comprehensive and fair faculty salary structure. While it may be expensive to understand an institution's current salary structure, it can be a great deal more expensive not to understand the institution's current salary structure.

Final Reminder

Correlation and other mathematical models do not prove causation, they simply describe the ability to explain differences within some statistical assumptions. Sufficiency and salience can be as compelling as statistical significance.

References

Academe. (2001). The Annual Report on the economic status of the profession 2000-2001.

Americans with Disabilities Act of 1990 and Section 504 of the Vocational Rehabilitation Act of 1973 http://www.usdoj.gov/crt/ada/adahom1.htm

Becker, W. E. and Toutkoushian, R, K. (1999, October 29). *Measuring gender bias in the salaries of tenured faculty members.* NBER Conference on Higher Education, Boston, MA.

Bickel, J., Croft, K. and Marshall, R. (1996). *Working toward salary equity.* Chapter 5. Enhancing the environment for women in academic medicine. Washington, DC: AAMC. http://www.aamc.org/members/wim/wimguide/

Blum, D., (1989) *Colleges worry that newly hired professors earn higher salaries than faculty veterans.* Chronicle of Higher Education, 36(7). (pp. A1, 21).

Boudreau, N., Sullivan, J., Balzer, W., Ryan, A. M., Yonker, R., Thorsteinson, T., and Hutchinson, P. (1997). *Should faculty rank be included as a predictor variable in studies of gender equity in university faculty salaries.* Research in Higher Education, Vol. 37. (pp. 633-658).

Braskamp, L. A. and Johnson, D. R. (1978). *The use of a parity-equity model to evaluate faculty salary policies,* Research in Higher Education, Vol. 8. (pp. 57-66).

Breneman, D. W., and Youn, T. I. K. (Eds.) (1988). Academic labor markets and careers. Philadelphia, PA: The Farmer Press.

Burton, C. (1998). *Gender equity in Australian university staffing* at http://www.wel.org.au/burton/ and at the Women's Electoral Lobby Australia Inc. http://www.wel.org.au/issues/

Brown University. (1996). 1996 Self Study, *Standard Five,* http:// www.brown.edu/Administration/Accreditation/standards/standard5.html

Brozovsky, P. V. and McLaughlin, G. W. (1994). *Issues in studying administrative faculty salary equity.* Paper presented at SAIR. San Antonio, TX.

California Postsecondary Education Commission. (1990). Faculty salaries in California's public universities, 1990-91 (Report 90-10). Sacramento, CA. http://www.cpec.ca.gov/HigherEdUpdates/Update2000/UP00-1.ASP

California Postsecondary Education Commission. (2001). Meeting Agenda for Monday and Tuesday, April 2-3, 2001. Report on Part-Time Faculty Compensation in California Community Colleges. http://www.cpec.ca.gov/commission/agnd0104.asp

Calhoun Community College. (2001). http://www.calhoun.cc.al.us/handbook/Chapter3.html#I

Civil Rights Act of 1964. Title VII. (2002). http://www.aristotle.net/~hantley/hiedlegl/statutes/title7/protclas.htm

Department of Justice. (2002). Age Discrimination in Employment Act of 1967 and the Older Workers Benefit Protection Act. (Public Law 101-433). (2002). http://hcl.chass.ncsu.edu/garson/dye/docs/adea.htm http://www.eeoc.gov/facts/age.html

Executive Order 11246. (2002). http://www.dol.gov/dol/esa/public/regs/compliance/ofccp/fs11246.htm

Equal Pay Act of 1963. (2002). http://www.aristotle.net/~hantley/hiedlegl/statutes/eqpay63.htm

Finkelstein, M. O. (1979, August). *The judicial reception of multiple regression studies in race and sex discrimination cases.* In Proceedings of the Social Statistics Section. Washington, D.C.: American Statistical Association.

Gray, M. W. and Scott, E. I. (1980). *A statistical remedy for statistically identified discrimination.* Academe, 66. (pp. 174-181).

Haignere, L. (2002). Paychecks: A guide to conducting salary equity studies for higher education faculty. Washington, DC: American Association of University Professors.

Hamermesh, D. (1988, May-June). *Salaries: Disciplinary differences and rank injustices.* Academe.

Harrigan, M. (1999). *Analysis of gender equity in 1997 faculty salaries at UW-Madison.* http://wiscinfo.doit.wisc.edu/obpa/GenderEquity/facultysalaries1997.html

Hinkel, D. E., Austin, J. T., and McLaughlin, G. W. (1989). *Log-linear models: applications in higher education research*. Higher Education: Handbook of Theory and Research. (pp. 323-353).

Hostler S. (1996). *Guidelines for planning a salary equity study*. In J. Bickel, K. Croft, and R. Marshall. (Eds.) Enhancing the environment for women in academic medicine, Appendix 5A.
http://www.aamc.org/members/wim/wimguide/wimapp5a.pdf

Howard, R. D., Snyder, J. K., and McLaughlin, G. W. (1992). *Faculty salaries.* In M A Whitney, J. D. Porter, and R. H. Fenske. (Eds.) The primer for institutional research. Tallahassee, FL: Association for Institutional Research.

Indiana State University. (2000, December 14). Faculty Senate Minutes.
http://www.senate.indstate.edu/Minutes/minutes%2F00-01

International Women's Site. (2002).
http://www-unix.umbc.edu/~korenman/wmst/links.html (copy and paste)

Lewis and Clark State College. (2001). Budget Priority Recommendations FY 2001 and FY 2002, Exempt Staff Committee. http://www.lcsc.edu/exemptstaff/BudgetPriority200102.htm

McCabe, G. P. (1979, August). *The interpretation of regression analysis results in sex and race discrimination problems.* Proceedings of the Social Statistics Section. Washington, D.C.: American Statistical Association.

McKee, P. (1997, Winter). *The Role of Institutional Research.* In Larry G. Jones. (Ed.). New Directions for Institutional Research: No. 96. Dealing with the complexities of higher education and law: An attorney's perspective in preventing lawsuits. San Francisco, CA: Jossey-Bass. (pp. 61-69).

McLaughlin, G. W., Howard, R. D., Balkan, L. A., and Blythe, E. W. (1998). People, Processes, and Managing Data. Tallahassee, FL: Association for Institutional Research.

McLaughlin, G. W., Frost, J. L. and Schultz, M. F. (1995). *Developing a strategic plan for implementing faculty salary adjustments.* Paper presented at the SCUP Annual Meeting, San Antonio, TX.

McLaughlin, G. W., Montgomery J. R., and Mahan, B. T. (1979). *Pay, rank, and growing old with more of each.* Research in Higher Education, 11(1). (pp. 23-35).

McLaughlin, G. .W., Smart, J. C., and Montgomery, J. R. (1978). *Factors which comprise salary.* Research in Higher Education, 8(1). (pp. 67-82).

McLaughlin, G. W., Zirkes, M. B., and Mahan, B. T. (1983). *Multicollinearity and testing questions of sex equity..* Research in Higher Education, 19(3). (pp. 277-284).

Moore, K. M. and Amey, M. J. (1993). *Making sense of the dollars: Then costs and uses of faculty compensation,* ASHE-ERIC Higher Education Reports, No 5.

Moore, N. (1993). *Faculty salary equity, issues in regression model selection.* Research In Higher Education, 34. (pp. 107-126).

National Center for Educational Statistics. (1994). National Study of Postsecondary Faculty. Washington, DC: NCES, US Department of Education. (pp. 94-346).

Neumann, Y. (1978). *Predicting faculty job satisfaction in university departments.* Research In Higher Education, Vol. 9. (pp. 261-275).

Newmark, D. (1988). *Employers' discriminatory behavior and the estimation of wage discrimination.* Journal of Human Resources, 23 (3). (pp. 279-295).

Oaxaca, R. (1973). *Male-female wage differentials in urban labor markets.* International Economic Review, 14(3). (pp. 693-709).

Office of Planning and Budget. (1999). *Faculty Salary Condition and Compression, IB99-9*, University of Missouri System. http://www.system.missouri.edu/planning/Issue_Brief/IB99-9/ib99-9.html

Ontario Ministry of Finance. (2001). Public Sector Salary Disclosure under the Public Sector Salary Disclosure Act of 1996. http://www.gov.on.ca/fin/english/psecteng.htm http://www.gov.on.ca/fin/english/unive01.pdf

Ourworld. (2002). Compuserve. http://ourworld.compuserve.com/homepages/PZarembka/aged.htm

Paulsen, M. B. (2000). *Economic perspectives on rising college tuition: A theoretical and empirical exploration.* In J. C. Smart and W. G. Tierney. (Eds.). Higher Education: Handbook of Theory and Research, Vol. XV. New York, NY: Agathon Press. (pp. 39-104).

Research Associates of Washington. (2001). *Higher education price index: Inflation measures for schools and colleges.* Washington, DC: http://www.rschassoc.com/

Scott, E. (1977). Higher education salary evaluation kit. American Association of University Professors.

Seattle Chamber of Commerce (2002). *Cost of Living Index.* http://www.seattlechamber.com/infocenter/almanac_costofliving.cfm

Smart, J. C. and McLaughlin, G. W. (1978). *Reward structures of academic disciplines.* Research In Higher Education, Vol. 8. (pp. 39-55).

Snyder, J. K., Hyer, P., and McLaughlin, G. W. (1994). *Faculty salary equity: Issues and options.* Research in Higher Education, Vol. 35, No. 1. (pp. 1-19).

Snyder, J. K., McLaughlin, G. W., and Montgomery, J. R. (1991). *Diagnosing and dealing with salary compression.* Research in Higher Education, Vol. 33, No. 1. (pp. 113-124).

Stapleton, L. M. (1999). *An alternative to the use of multiple regression to evaluate faculty salary equity.* Paper presented at the AIR Forum, Seattle, WA.

Status of Women in Canada. (2002). http://www.swc-cfc.gc.ca

Swiss Statistics. (2002). *National Consumer Price Index.* http://www.statistik.admin.ch/stat_ch/ber05/eu0501.htm

Teeter, D. J. and Brinkman, P. T. (1992). *Peer Institutions.* In M. A. Whitney, J. D. Porter and R. H. Fenske. (Eds.). The primer for institutional research, Association for Institutional Research. (pp. 63-72).

Terenzini P. T. (1993). *On the nature of institutional research and the knowledge and skills it requires.* Research In Higher Education, Vol. 34(1). (pp. 1-10).

Toutkoushian, R. K. (1994a). *Issues in choosing a strategy for achieving salary equity.* Research in Higher Education, Vol. 35, 4. (pp. 415-427).

Toutkoushian, R. K. (1994b). *Using citations to measure sex discrimination in faculty salaries.* The Review of Higher Education, Vol. 18, no 1. (pp. 61-82).

Toutkoushian, R. K. (1998). *Sex matters less for younger faculty: Evidence of disaggregate pay disparities from the 1988 and 1993 NCES surveys.* Economics of Education Review, Vol. 17, (1). (pp. 55-71).

Toutkoushian, R. K. (1999). *The status of academic women in the 1990's: No longer outsiders, but not yet equals.* The Quarterly Review of Economics and Finance, Vol. 39. (pp. 679-698).

Toutkoushian, R. K. (2000). *Addressing gender equity in nonfaculty salaries.* Research in Higher Education, Vol. 41. (pp. 417-442).

University of Wisconsin – Madison. (2000). Office of the Provost, *Women Faculty and Staff Issues, 2000/2001 gender pay equity review.* http://www.wisc.edu/provost/GEFS.html

University of Louisville. (1999, July). Faculty Senate Meeting Minutes. http://www.louisville.edu/gov/facultysenate/sm070799.htm

University of Oregon. (2000, March 15). *University Senate Budget Committee White Paper: A plan for sustained competitive parity in instructional faculty compensation.* http://www.uoregon.edu/~uosenate/dirsen990/SBCfinal.html

Virginia. (2002). http://legis.state.va.us/codecomm/valac/foiaview.htm

Wenger, R. B. and Girard, D. M. (2000). *A faculty merit pay allocation model.* Research in Higher Education, Vol. 41, No. 2. (pp. 195-207).

Women's Electoral Lobby Australia, Inc. (2002). http://www.wel.org.au/issues/

Yuker, H. E. (1984). *Faculty workload: Research, theory, and interpretation.* (ERIC Document Reproduction Service No. ED 259 691).

End Notes

[1] The references following this chapter provide descriptions of methodologies required in the conduct of salary equity studies.

[2] See Toutkoushian,(1998) for an extension of this discussion, as well as a comparison of Newmark, Oaxaca, and other methods.

[3] If you choose to use this approach, you might want to review the work of Stapleton (1999) in which Hieratical Linear Modeling was used with clusters of disciplines and then salaries were modeled with the variation of some measures allowed between discipline clusters.

Chapter 5
Enrollment Management

Richard J. Kroc, University of Arizona
Gary Hanson, Arizona State University

Introduction

When asked to define enrollment management, many college faculty and administrators will point toward the admissions office and say, "It's what those admissions folks do—get us the students." While recruiting students is clearly part of managing college enrollments, much more is at stake. Writers and practitioners have proposed several more comprehensive definitions for enrollment management. For example, Kemerer, Baldridge and Green (1982) suggest that enrollment management is both a process and a series of activites, involving the entire campus. Clagett (1992) describes enrollment management as "the coordinated effort of a college or university to influence the size and characteristics of the institution's student body." Using a broader and more inclusive definition, Hossler, Bean and Associates (1990) define enrollment management as activities and issues involving student college choice, transition to college, student attrition and retention, and student outcomes.

Enrollment management, for the purpose of this chapter, is defined as an institutional research and planning function that examines, and seeks to manage, the flow of students to, through, and from college. This chapter views the enterprise chronologically, from the time a student becomes a prospect to the time they exit or become an alumnus. Two primary domains, student recruitment and student flow, have been identified, partly because colleges tend to organize their offices and resources somewhat separately around these two areas and partly because much of the writing about enrollment management has considered recruitment and retention separately. This chapter uses the term "student flow," rather than retention, to make the case for widening that domain somewhat. Student recruitment has been divided into the educational pipeline (marketing and recruitment), enrollment projections, and financial aid. In the student flow domain, areas and issues include academic preparation, the curriculum, academic support programs, retention, and alumni. While the assessment of student learning should be an integral part of enrollment management, this discussion has been intentionally limited. For further discussion on assessment of student learning, see Chapter 2 of this volume.

In addition to exploring many of the important enrollment management issues, this chapter considers how colleges can best address enrollment needs and how institutional researchers can help. How should the institution organize for enrollment management? What technical skills are needed? How can data best be collected and organized? How can the researcher best communicate results? This chapter has two goals:

- To provide a richer understanding of the important enrollment management issues.

- To help campuses and institutional researchers move from reacting to enrollments to managing them.

STUDENT RECRUITMENT
The Educational Pipeline

The process of student recruitment begins with two important questions: "Who does the institution want to educate?" and "Who is available?" Defining who the institution wants to educate is a product of the institution's mission and goals; however, these goals must be moderated with an understanding of how many students exist in the potential pipeline. Student recruitment is an expensive business. Pursuing enrollment goals beyond the available pipeline is frustrating, as well as a waste of precious institutional resources. The end goal is to identify, attract, enroll, and graduate students.

While the pipeline of potential students may vary from one institution to the next, defining the boundaries of the educational pipeline for the institution is an important task for effective student recruitment. To define these boundaries for the educational pipeline, a researcher must ask, "What are the defining characteristics of the students the institution wants to recruit?" The next step is to identify data sources that summarize how many pre-college students with those characteristics exist in the pipeline: that is, who is available. This process starts with a broad global picture of who is included in the higher education educational pipeline. A more refined definition of the recruitment pool is then needed and should begin with a discussion of the desired characteristics of the students that the institution wishes to enroll.

Understanding Student Choice

Understanding how students chose a college is an important aspect of recruiting students (Hossler, Schmitz and Vespar, 1999). Institutional researchers may be asked to:

- Conduct marketing studies that determine what factors influence students to apply, become admitted, and enroll at the institution.

- Identify databases and software analysis tools that facilitate the institution's ability to locate, recruit, and attract students in the pipeline. Both the College Board and the American College Testing Program provide access to data and sell lists of students who meet specific educational criteria.

- Generate a trend analysis that compares characteristics of this year's applicants with applicants from previous years at the same point in time.

- Compare admitted students who ultimately chose to enroll with those who did not.

- Provide institutional data to college ranking services such as *U.S. News and World Report*, *Peterson's Guide*, and *The College Blue Book*.

- Provide data about student and parental perceptions of the institution's image as compared with data from other institutions.

Yield Rates

Understanding enrollment yield is one of the most critical issues associated with the intersection of the educational pipeline and student enrollment. "Yield rates" refer to ratios among the numbers of students who apply, are admitted, and enroll at an institution. The analysis of yield rates involves a comparison of those who applied, were admitted, and enrolled with those who did not. It should also include comparing trends from the current year with previous years, often using three, five or 10 year rolling averages.

This trend analysis provides an important context for evaluating the effectiveness of recruitment activities or changes in admissions policy. If the number of applications either declines or increases several years in a row, significant changes in the educational pipeline for the institution may be evident. Similar changes across multiple student target groups will inform campus administrators about changes in the pipeline or the effectiveness of various recruiting activities aimed at these student groups. Two indicators are important to monitor: the *admit yield rate* and the *enrollment yield rate*. The *admit yield rate* is the percentage of applicants who were admitted. This indicator is a function of institutional admissions policy. Changing the admissions policy will change the *admit yield rate*. The second indicator is the *enrollment yield rate*. This indicator is the percentage of admitted students who enroll and is a function of the students' decisions to enroll at the institution or to attend another institution.

To accomplish these analyses, the institutional research office must establish student tracking systems that capture student behavior during the recruitment, admission, and matriculation stages of college enrollment. These tracking systems may be developed locally or purchased from commercial vendors. Data warehousing and data mining software may be used to answer specific individual faculty and staff queries; however, the development and maintenance of these tracking systems may fall within the duties of the institutional research office. A variety of statistical techniques may be used for analyses. For example, a new technique imported from cognitive psychology, artificial neural networks, looks promising (Byers-Gonzalez and Desjardins, 2001).

Enrollment Projections

Projecting college enrollments can be a difficult, even perilous, activity. The stakes can be high in terms of budgetary, facilities planning, and instructional concerns, yet projections are often not as accurate as hoped or expected. Before a researcher engages in this process, several questions should be addressed:

- What are the needs of the institution?

- What are the dimensions of the analysis (variables and levels of analysis)?

- What is the time horizon?

- What methodology should be used?

- How should qualitative and quantitative input be balanced?

A thorough grasp of the needs and context for enrollment projections is essential to successfully completing the project. The institutional needs that should be considered range from the budgetary process, to faculty demand and classroom space, to facilities management, to the recruitment activities of the admissions and financial aid offices.

Timing is a critical dimension in creating enrollment projections. Useful distinctions can be made between short-term and long-term projections. Budgeting, instructional planning, and student recruitment generally need two to three year projections. Strategic planning and facilities management require longer term forecasts, often 10 years or more into the future.

A variety of quantitative methods can be used for projecting enrollments. Brinkman and McIntyre (1997) compare and contrast many of these methods, providing useful descriptions of strengths and weaknesses. They discuss curve-fitting techniques, causal models, and student flow analysis.

Quantitative approaches may have limited utility for long-term projections. An alternative, scenario development, can provide a much richer sense of long-term possibilities. Scenarios are designed to be a planning tool that develops a set (usually 3-5) of plausible future stories, or scenes, that a linear projection of the past may not anticipate. A scenario "describes a situation in common terms that represents what might happen in the future. It is not a prediction, but a way of putting a lot of ideas and possibilities together" (Caldwell, 1999). These are not simply a researcher's momentary visions, but are based on a solid understanding of social, technological, environmental, economic, and political issues (Morrison, 1992).

Although quantitative methods can be accurate and useful, particularly for short-term projections, they may often be improved by incorporating other, more subjective, information. It can be very valuable to have an enrollment management committee to add expert judgment to the initial quantitative modeling. These informed judgments can add critical information regarding why, and how much, enrollments may deviate from the projections.

Financial Aid

As college costs have risen in recent years, financial aid has become a critical aspect of enrollment management. Both colleges and students are increasingly dependent on "discounting" tuition and fees by using financial aid resources. Although private colleges have been grappling with financial aid issues for many years, public institutions often find themselves in unfamiliar territory, as their dependence on student aid escalates.

Understanding the Issues and Data

Close collaboration with the financial aid office is essential to successful enrollment management. Of all the enrollment management areas, financial aid provides the greatest challenges with regard to the retrieval and analysis of data, as well as the complexity of issues.

A number of questions can help guide the analyst exploring this area:

- What is the college's student financial aid policy? Who determines the policy? How well integrated are the admissions and the student financial aid policies?

- What types of aid are available? How do students qualify?

- How is aid packaged? How and when are students offered aid? How is it disbursed?

- How are gift aid, loans and employment balanced?

- How are the recruitment and retention functions of aid balanced?

- What are some of the basic aid statistics reported by the aid office?

  - How many students receive aid? New students? Continuing students?

  - How many receive gift aid? Loans? Employment?

  - How many receive need-based aid? How many show unmet need?

  - How much aid is disbursed? What is the net tuition revenue?

  - What is the price of attendance?

  - What is the level of student indebtedness?

  - How do these statistics vary by student subgroup?

  - What are the trends over time?

Sources of Information

For the institutional researcher investigating student financial aid, several sources provide valuable information. The *New Directions for Institutional Research* series has published *Researching Student Aid: Creating an Action Agenda* (Voorhees, ed., 1997), while the National Association of Student Financial Aid Administrators has published *Student Aid Research: A Manual for Financial Aid Administrators* (Davis, ed., 1997). These two publications include important background information about financial aid issues and suggest useful approaches for research studies. They also discuss national databases that may be valuable to the analyst. In addition, the *Postsecondary Education Opportunity* newsletter, published monthly by Tom Mortenson, addresses critical aid, funding, and access issues, often providing useful comparative data for all 50 states. Finally, the

National Association of State Student Aid and Grant Programs sponsors an annual conference focused entirely on student aid research. This conference provides cutting edge research presentations and access to a national network of financial aid researchers.

National Concerns

Frequently, institutional researchers are asked to provide local policy analyses related to a number of national concerns regarding student financial aid. Understanding these issues provides a foundation for managing enrollment. A brief list of national concerns is offered here:

- The interplay between financial aid and college prices, especially tuition
- The impact of federal and state policies on financial aid
- Use of financial aid leveraging for more effective student recruitment
- The rapid escalation of student loans and student indebtedness

The interested reader may consult Kroc and Hanson (2001) for a more detailed description.

STUDENT FLOW
Academic Preparation

Student flow through an institution begins with the selection of students. This is the point at which recruitment and retention merge. The institution may admit everyone who applies; more commonly, however, the choice regarding who is admitted depends on the academic readiness of students to attend college. Indicators of academic readiness have been used in two very different ways to facilitate enrollment management decisions regarding student flow into and through college: 1) selection for college admission, and 2) placement into appropriate courses.

Selecting Students

At the very heart of enrollment management is the identification, recruitment, and admission of qualified students. What characterizes a qualified student? The answer may be found in the mission statement of every campus. Whether to consider the academic preparation of students in the enrollment management process depends on several issues. First, does the institution need to be selective? Can the institution afford to admit all students who apply, or must it limit the numbers who enroll? If enrollment must be limited, on what basis will students be selected? How much emphasis should be placed on measures of academic preparation relative to other student characteristics, such as age, gender, leadership ability, socioeconomic status, ability-to-pay, or racial/ethnic background?

Historically, two measures of academic preparation have been used in making selection decisions. First, colleges and universities use measures of academic performance in high school, such as relative class rank or average grade point average, over a selected number of courses. Second, standardized measures of academic ability, such as the Scholastic Ability Test (SAT) or the American College Testing Program (ACT) tests, are used to supplement measures of high school performance.

Do measures of academic preparation select the "best" students? Both measures of high school performance and standardized test scores are related in significant ways to the academic performance of students in college (ACT, 2000). In fact, during the last 50 years, high school performance and standardized tests typically account for about 25 pecent to 40 percent of the variance in college grades. These measures consistently do better than almost any other indicator of student preparation. However, academic performance is only one of the ways to define the "best" students. There is much that these measures do not tell us about the nature of college student success.

The research literature shows that high school rank or high school grade point average in combination with a standardized test score consistently do the best job of predicting college grade point average and retention during the first year. They do not, however, work as well predicting subsequent academic performance. They also do a relatively poor job of predicting who will graduate after four, five or six years. These measures also fail to predict important student measures of success, such as leadership ability, writing ability, analytical thinking, or the ability to work as a team member. Institutional researchers are often asked to conduct analyses to understand how the criteria used to select students are related to subsequent outcomes, such as academic performance or graduation.

Placing Students

Enrollment managers first select students for college, then must place them into the "right" level of a particular course. Poor placement can diminish the flow of students from entry-level courses to more advanced courses and, eventually, to graduation. Measures of academic preparation are used widely for placing students into courses. Often, the same measures are used both to select and to place students. While students may have sufficiently high test scores, and/or high school rank/gpa, to be admitted to a given institution, they may not meet the faculty standards for the preparation needed to benefit from instruction in a particular course. Hence, measures of academic preparation more closely tied to course content, such as achievement tests, are needed to make these placement decisions for enrollment managers. Local faculty may construct these achievement tests, or the institution may purchase commercial tests. In some institutions, the college admissions test, such as ACT or SAT, are used as a proxy measure that closely approximates what will be taught in the curriculum.

The effectiveness with which measures of academic preparation help enrollment managers place students appropriately can be evaluated using three indicators. First, how many of the students expected to pass their courses do so? Second, how many of the students judged to be "ready" for a particular course fail the course? Finally, how many of the students judged to be under-prepared could have successfully completed a more difficult course without taking the prerequisite course?

Other Academic Assets

Students today are more diverse in their level of preparation. Fewer students who pursue college have completed a "college-prep" curriculum. Consequently, the traditional standardized test scores and grade point averages may not provide all the necessary information regarding student preparation. Adelman (1999) argued that the best indicators of academic performance and eventual graduation from college for today's college students are the intensity and the patterns of coursework completed in high school, rather than the more traditional measures. Completing demanding courses in several subjects may be more important than receiving a high grade or class rank in less difficult courses.

In addition to better understanding the rigor and the intensity of involvement with demanding high school course work, other indicators of accomplishment that students bring with them to college should be examined. College faculty want students who can write and who have increasingly higher levels of computer literacy. Business and industry leaders want students who can work together in teams, show leadership initiative, and can work with others from diverse backgrounds. To meet these demands, our definition of academic preparation must expand beyond our traditional measures of high school performance and standardized test score.

The Curriculum

The curriculum is at the heart of the student college experience. A comprehensive program of enrollment management research logically should include a systematic examination of the impact of the curriculum, yet this is not often done. In this chapter, the term student flow is used, rather than retention, to expand the enrollment management domain to include such studies. Immensely improved administrative systems and data warehouses, coupled with much higher speed computers, make studying the impact of the curriculum on student retention and graduation within easier reach.

Types of Studies

Conversations with faculty and academic administrators can be a particularly useful way to identify the curricular studies that would be most valuable to the institution. For example, analyzing the impact of gatekeeping, or gateway, courses on student progress can result in valuable information and stimulate useful campus discussion. These are the key courses, often with high failure rates, that control the flow of lower division students into higher levels of study. There are a number of issues to be addressed regarding these courses, including the number and characteristics of students who fail, the impact of failure on retention, the impact of performance in these courses on subsequent courses, and trends over time. We refer the reader to studies by Andrade (1999) and materials from panel presentations at the 1998 and 1999 Association for Institutional Research (AIR) Annual Forums available at http://www.airweb.org.

Closely related to gateway course studies are analyses of grading practices. Some institutions have found that course grade distributions in gateway courses have not changed over a period of years, even though student high school preparation may have markedly improved (Hanson, Norman & Caillouet, 1998). Moreover, the failure rate in individual course sections may vary greatly, even after controlling for initial preparation. On the other hand, institutions are also greatly concerned about grade inflation and about courses where all students receive grades of "A." Examining grading practices and patterns can be a perilous pursuit, because the analysis may raise questions about the validity of faculty assessment of students.

Academic advising, choice of a major, and course availability have also become topics of increasing importance. At large public Research I universities, a recent study (Kroc, et al, 1997) determined that 72 percent of those students who initially chose a major changed that major before they graduated. Peter Ewell has used the term *behavioral curriculum* to distinguish how students actually navigate the curriculum, as opposed to what they are asked and expected to do. Behavioral curriculum issues offer fruitful territory for curricular studies. Interrupting attendance or taking courses out of sequence are examples of behaviors that may adversely affect grades and retention. Another example is taking the relevant prerequisite course too far in advance of a higher level course.

The link between student outcomes assessment and enrollment management should be particularly strong in the area of student flow through the curriculum. A good assessment program not only provides valuable data, including other dependent variables to use for research studies, but will also establish a feedback loop in which assessment results are used to inform faculty and to improve the curriculum. Developing collaborative research in this area can be fruitful, if another office is responsible for student assessment.

Campus Climate

The curriculum exists within the overall campus environment or climate. The assessment of campus climate is an important function for institutional researchers (Bauer, 1998). Increasingly, administrators want to monitor what students think about the campus atmosphere. The assessment of campus climate is important because attitudes about the institutional climate may influence enrollment behavior at three critical points in time. First, institutional image attracts or repels students early in the college choice process. Second, students' perceptions of the campus climate also influence their final choice of institutions. Typically, students narrow their college choice to a small, select list of colleges or universities. The institutional climate and the institution's reputation are critical factors when making their final choice. Third, once students arrive on campus, the day-to-day campus climate sets the boundaries of involvement the student has with the institution. The student will be more likely to leave if the campus climate interferes with the bond between the student and the college. On the other hand, when students find the campus climate attractive, the student develops a level of commitment to the institution. He or she will then be more likely to successfully navigate the curriculum.

It may be advisable for the researcher to pursue a different paradigm of inquiry if the assessment of campus climate is just beginning at an institution, in order to identify the important defining issues on campus. This can be accomplished through a qualitative study, using individual or group interviews or focus groups. One example of this mode of inquiry by Seymour and Hewitt (1997) studies the classroom climates that facilitated, or hindered, women and minority students' pursuit of science, mathematics, and engineering majors in college.

Academic and Student Support Programs

Higher education institutions spend considerable time and money, over and beyond the cost of classroom instruction, to improve student learning. Because the investment of time and money is substantial, colleges and universities often ask institutional researchers to evaluate the effectiveness of these programs. How can it be determined whether these academic and student support services contribute to student learning and success? The evaluation issues can be discussed in the context of formative and summative evaluation. Evaluating the effectiveness in achieving the program's goals and objectives is called summative evaluation. Evaluating the process by which the program was delivered is called formative evaluation.

Formative or Process Evaluation

Every program begins with intentions regarding how the program should be delivered, to whom and when. The evaluation process begins with written specifications regarding the intended process. Next, evidence must be collected from program developers and participants to determine whether or not the intended program was really delivered. Another important step in process evaluation is the analysis of whether or not the target group of students attended the program. Keeping accurate records, using technology to monitor participation and building databases to link participation to critical outcome information is highly important. Student satisfaction with how the program was delivered must also be assessed. Was it timely, well organized, and delivered with appropriate methodology? Finally, process evaluation involves asking participants whether improvements could be made to the way the program was delivered. The current participants are the experts for improving the program for the next generation of participants.

Summative or Outcome Evaluation

One of the most difficult program evaluation issues is determining whether or not a particular effort produces learning outcomes over and beyond that expected, after careful examination of the student's level of academic preparation, motivation, and readiness for college. The evaluator must collect appropriate evidence regarding these student characteristics and choose analytic techniques, such as hierarchical linear regression models to statistically account for pre-program characteristics students bring to the program. The important question is whether student learning occurred over and above these initial student characteristics.

Another important aspect of summative evaluation is determining whether or not participants achieved the desired outcomes at better rates than non-participants. Hence, the evaluator must identify students with similar background characteristics to the program participants to include in a comparative analysis. When matched samples are not available, sophisticated research designs and statistical analyses are often necessary to provide an accurate portrayal of the situation. See Kroc and Hanson (2001) for suggested analysis strategies.

Isolating the effects of a given academic or student support program is one of the most difficult outcome evaluation issues. The problem is that students live complicated lives; they participate in many activities that may potentially influence their learning, retention, and graduation. They often participate in these activities simultaneously; therefore, isolating the effect of a single program within the context of all other programs can be very difficult. Assumptions that students only participate in one program may result in the attribution of the effects of one program to another. The use of a multiple program impact evaluation strategy (Hanson & Swann, 1993) can counter this problem. By tracking student participation in multiple programs during a given semester, not only can the effect of a single program be determined, but the combined effect of multiple participation over and beyond the effects of any single program can also be evaluated.

Finally, when conducting summative evaluations, it is important to ask whether the program contributed to the broader mission of the institution. For example, many retention programs are effective for small groups of students, but the institutional graduation rate never improves. While the program works, its impact on the broader mission is insignificant because too few students participate, educational policy negates the long-term effect of the program, or other events later in the students' academic career interfere with the positive contribution of the program. The ability to link the impact of the program to the mission of the institution is extremely important, but rarely is the effectiveness of programs evaluated relative to this criterion.

Institutional researchers can help their colleagues determine if academic and student support services accomplish important institutional and program goals. Gathering and analyzing information helps program developers examine the process and the outcome of their efforts. Collecting data for both purposes may avoid the pitfalls of conducting program evaluations that identify problems but offer no viable solutions for improvement. By summarizing data about the success of the program, and how to improve it for future delivery, institutional researchers will have provided a valuable service.

Graduation and Retention Rates

Surveys show that graduation and retention rates are the most frequently used indicators in state level accountability and performance measure initiatives. The federal government has also begun to require reporting of graduation rate data. As a result, virtually all institutions are now able to produce graduation rate data. Turning this accountability data into information useful for managing enrollments, however, requires some thoughtfulness on the part of the institutional researcher. A few of the important current issues facing colleges and universities are:

- Increasing the institution's retention and graduation rates

- Increasing transfer rates and baccalaureate degree completion of community college students

- Reducing time-to-graduation

- Closing the gap between underrepresented groups and other students

- Increasing academic preparation—the link between recruitment and retention

- Implementing and evaluating efficient and effective retention programs

Descriptive Data

Efficiency and flexibility are two fundamental requirements for a useful system to analyze graduation rates. Ewell (1995) describes student tracking systems in detail. Such systems allow the researcher to track cohorts of students over time, as they progress through the institution.

Survey data can be a valuable adjunct to institutional data about attrition. Students who have recently withdrawn from an institution can provide useful feedback about their current situation, reasons for leaving, attitudes, and plans. It is very important for comparative purposes to also survey students who have returned. This permits the researcher to profile the similarities and differences between those who stay and those who leave.

Multivariate Analyses

Retention is a subtle and complex issue with many different determinants, which sometimes may be best understood using multivariate analyses. Perhaps the best known example of this approach is Astin's (1993) work, which examined the predictability of graduation rates from entry characteristics of students in light of his tri-partite model: input, environment, and outcome. Astin advocated computing a predicted graduation rate, which could then be compared with an institution's actual rate as an assessment of performance. Mortenson (1997) modified this approach using a different set of predictors not within the control of institutions, then using the results to rank states, as well as individual institutions, based on differences between predicted and actual graduation rates.

Causal modeling, also known as path analysis or structural equation modeling, has been useful to some researchers as a method to more accurately identify causal relationships among complex, interrelated data. In recent years, most volumes of *Research in Higher Education* contain examples of this method. Hazard or survival analysis, a relatively new method imported into higher education from medicine, promises to further refine and improve our analysis of graduation rates. DesJardins, Ahlberg and McCall (1999), for example, have used this method to better understand the temporal dimensions of first stopout or dropout.

Qualitative Methods

Although most retention studies use quantitative methods, qualitative approaches can be valuable in some situations, revealing issues and providing insights that will be otherwise missed. In situations where little is known, perhaps with small populations of students, these methods (interviews, case studies, ethnographies or participant observation, for example) can be particularly useful. These situations should be carefully selected, because these approaches are labor intensive. Some administrators may also have serious misgivings about crafting policy from the small number of cases studied in most qualitative research. For an excellent example of this methodology see Seymour and Hewitt (1997).

Peer Data

In addition to understanding local concerns, the researcher needs to be informed about the national context. A number of sources for national graduation rate data now exist. One of the best is *the Consortium for Student Retention Data Exchange* (Smith, 1999), which provided data for 269 United States colleges and universities in 1999. Many groups of institutions now have data exchanges (for example, the AAU Data Exchange) to facilitate the sharing of more detailed information. In the age of attachments and electronic files, informal collaborations among institutions facing similar issues can be fruitful and engaging. Use e-mail or the *Electronic AIR* to begin a conversation with colleagues.

Beyond Graduation

Consistent with the student flow perspective, enrollment management should not end when students graduate or transfer. Valuable insights can be gained from alumni, as well as from employers. Comprehensive surveys of alumni have become widespread among colleges and universities, partly as a result of assessment and accountability pressures. Much can be learned from these surveys about former students' employment, continuing education, location, satisfaction with their educational experiences and career preparation.

Employers are another group that can provide valuable feedback. Periodic surveys of employers can be used to gather data for student assessment, accountability, and enrollment management needs. Such information might include:

- The overall quality and training of an institution's graduates/students

- The preparation of graduates in specific areas, such as writing skills, technical skills, quantitative reasoning, oral communication, leadership, and teamwork

- The accessibility of the campus, and its students, to the employer for interviewing

- Trends in past hiring and expectations for the future

SUPPORTING ENROLLMENT MANAGEMENT
Organizing for Enrollment Management

The most elegant analyses will lie fallow unless an effective institutional structure exists for managing enrollments. Several components need to be interwoven to create an environment where good ideas can be implemented and necessary changes are fostered. These components include campus planning, the functional units responsible for implementing changes, institutional research, and administrative support.

Enrollment management and enrollment planning can be thought of as synonymous. Enrollment management can fail if it becomes separated from other campus planning activities, particularly if these activities involve budgeting and facilities. A certain amount of education, and perhaps change management, may be needed to persuade key campus constituencies that enrollment issues are pervasive in their impact on the entire campus. Drawing on professional literature regarding enrollment management (Dennis, 1998; Hossler, Bean and Associates, 1990) can be helpful in infusing this broader perspective into campus discussions. These sources are useful for the institutional researcher, and they can also be very persuasive when placed in the right hands at an appropriate time. The national perspective reflected in these books, as well as in other publications and research studies, can be a critical element for educating the campus community and securing the administrative support needed to successfully integrate the enrollment management enterprise with the overall college planning processes.

Organizational Structures

Successful enrollment management structures come in all shapes and sizes. Some are centralized, some decentralized. Some depend on a hierarchical management structure; others invoke a flat structure. Some emanate from student affairs and others from academic affairs. The person or agency responsible for coordinating the enterprise might be the admissions director, a faculty member, the vice president for undergraduate education, the provost, or a committee. New and radically different structures can not easily be imposed in most cases. Changes need to be reasonably consistent with the existing organization, or they are likely to fail. Enrollment management is usually an evolutionary process, rather than one marked by sharp, sudden managerial change (Hossler, Bean and Associates, 1990).

Some useful ways to conceptualize and describe alternative approaches and organizational structures do exist. This section describes a framework that can help guide a college or university toward more effective strategies. Originally developed by Kemerer, Baldridge, and Green (1982) in their book *Strategies for Effective Enrollment Management*, this framework continues to be instructive for understanding alternative structures for managing college enrollments. They described four models: the enrollment management committee, the enrollment management coordinator, the enrollment management matrix, and the enrollment management division. Hossler (1990) also provides an excellent description of these models.

Technical and Analytic Skills

In his reflective article about the nature of institutional research, Pat Terenzini (1993) conceptualizes three tiers of organizational intelligence that need to be present for effective research: technical/analytic, issues, and contextual intelligence. Most of this chapter has been devoted to an overview of the second tier, the many issues involved in enrollment management. Some discussion of the third tier, which "involves understanding the culture both of higher education in general and of the particular campus where the institutional researcher works" (Terenzini, 1993, p.3), has also been included. This chapter would be incomplete, though, without some discussion of the first tier of organizational intelligence: the technical and analytical skills needed to undertake enrollment management research. Although this tier is insufficient by itself, it is "fundamental and foundational" (Terenzini, 1993, p.4) to the two higher level tiers and to an effective enrollment management program.

Factual Knowledge

With regard to the technical/analytical tier, Terenzini (1993) distinguishes factual knowledge, which is usually acquired on-the-job, from methodological skills, which are initially learned more formally from coursework. Characteristics of factual knowledge include familiarity with standard categories [e.g. prospective student, applicant, admitted student, matriculated student, alumnus, high school background characteristics (SAT/ACT scores, class rank, high school GPA, etc.) to name just a few]. Counting rules and formulae include calculating the number of FTE students, the price of education, students' grade point averages, costs per credit hour, student financial need, student/faculty ratios, and others. Although this type of knowledge can be learned from an institutional research and planning course, or from directed readings, most analysts acquire this content as dictated by their work responsibilities.

Methodological Skills

Knowledge of methodological skills is generally best acquired through formal coursework at the graduate level, most often in education or the social sciences. The methodological skills needed include research design, statistics, survey design and sampling, qualitative methods, psychometrics, and program evaluation.

A solid understanding of research design is the essential methodological foundation for the enrollment management analyst. When an enrollment question is posed, the analyst needs to have a working understanding of an array of research design strategies from which to choose. In many cases, more than one alternative may be possible; an informed choice can make the difference between a successful and unsuccessful outcome. Deciding between a survey or focus group approach, or using a matched pairs design instead of regression, for example, may be important. Because most higher education interventions create situations that are quasi-experimental in nature, the researcher needs to have a solid grasp of these techniques. Rarely is random assignment used to place students into retention programs, so comparing the control and experimental groups can be difficult. Fortunately, much has been written in this area. A good place to start is the classic text, *Quasi-Experimentation* (Cook and Campbell, 1979). While coursework and readings are the essential starting point for a mastery of research design, only the trial and error process of engaging in actual studies can complete the analyst's training.

The statistician has been scorned as a person who drowns in a river with an average depth of three feet. Nonetheless, a working understanding of statistics is also an important part of the analyst's arsenal. This understanding should begin with basic descriptive statistics and exploratory data analysis (Tukey, 1977). It should also include basic probability, inferential statistics, measurement error, hypothesis testing, and bivariate and multivariate techniques. Regression and structural equation modeling have become increasingly popular and valuable for analyzing retention outcomes. Although the analyst will want to bring the best statistical techniques to bear on an issue, too much statistical detail in a report or presentation can be distracting.

Survey design and sampling have also become increasingly important skills for the enrollment management analyst in recent years. Surveys are used to assess the reasons why students do not matriculate, why they withdraw, how they view instructors and the curriculum, and what their lives are like after graduation. Student outcomes assessment programs make particular use of surveys that may also be helpful for the enrollment analyst. Two useful sources for practical survey design information are *Mail and Internet Surveys: The Tailored Design Method* (Dillman, 2000) and the Association for Institutional Research book, *Questionnaire Survey Research: What Works* (Suskie, 1992).

Qualitative methods can be employed usefully by the enrollment manager, particularly in situations where little is known or where detailed and richly descriptive analysis is needed. This is more than a choice of methods; it is also an epistemological decision. Because of these philosophical differences, a debate continues about appropriate uses of these methods and about the wisdom of blending qualitative and quantitative methods in program evaluation or research studies. Hathaway (1995) has published an article for institutional researchers comparing and contrasting the two approaches and Fetterman (1991) has an excellent text on the subject. Because some issues lend themselves to these methods, and some stakeholders are very responsive to case studies and "thick description," enrollment analysts should consider using qualitative techniques more often.

A cursory understanding of measurement issues can also assist the enrollment analyst. Although enrollment studies are more likely to require the construction of affective scales, it can be useful even in the cognitive domain to understand reliability and validity issues, item analysis techniques, scaling, and other related concepts.

Interest in program evaluation has increased in recent years as the number of retention programs has grown. The *Academic and Student Support Programs* section of this chapter describes the value and process of program evaluation. *Evaluating with Validity* (House, 1980) also provides a sense for many of the issues and an excellent overview of evaluation.

Sometimes it is more efficient and effective to allow an outside firm to conduct the research. Educational Testing Service (ETS) and the ACT offer an array of services related to enrollment management and assessment. Noel-Levitz, and other firms, offer their services in the areas of retention and financial aid leveraging. Using outside sources should be seen as an adjunct to, rather than a substitute for, an in-house enrollment management program.

Data Sources

The analysis of enrollment management issues requires a wide array of data, both internal and external to the institution. Obtaining the data needed for an analysis can be a major obstacle. Simple, critical analyses are sometimes not possible because data are either unavailable or inadequate. Most institutional data is collected for purposes that may not be directly related to the needs of the enrollment management researcher. Admissions offices need to attract and admit students; financial aid offices need to disburse aid; the Bursar needs to collect tuition and fees, etc. Understanding how and why such offices do their business can be essential to understanding the data needed by the researcher but collected and controlled by other offices. Institutional researchers need to be on good terms with the offices on which they depend.

Peer Data and Performance Indicators

Peer data can provide valuable comparisons that help establish a context for strategic enrollment planning. A rich array of National Center for Education Statistics (NCES) Integrated Postsecondary Education Data Survey (IPEDS) data and reports is now available through their Web site (http://nces.ed.gov/). The accelerating need for information has also spawned a number of data exchanges and peer databases. The Association of American Universities Data Exchange, for example, provides data in a variety of areas to its member institutions. Some individual institutions have obtained funding to compile peer data, making their databases available to others through paper reports, Web sites, spreadsheets, CD-ROM, or some other means. The Consortium for Student Retention and Data Exchange (CSRDE) annually publishes student retention and graduation rates for its 330 members. The University of Delaware has compiled, analyzed, and widely distributed data about faculty workload and academic program costs. Finally, the data found in a variety of publications, such as *U.S. News and World Report* and *Peterson's Guide*, have become increasingly useful as sources for peer data. The Common Data Set, which many institutions update annually for use in these publications, has helped considerably to standardize and facilitate this process. In summary, peer data useful in meeting enrollment management needs has become more available and more useful.

Performance indicators are becoming increasingly common in higher education. Colleges and universities may need to establish sets of peer institutions and gather comparable peer data to interpret and analyze these indicators. Such data can be influential in statewide conversations about managing enrollments, particularly because governing boards and legislative staffs may be familiar with these indicators and more likely to use them (wisely or not) when crafting policy. In many states, student survey results and other assessment data are being used as performance indicators. On campuses where assessment is organizationally separated from institutional research, it may be important to become familiar with assessment activities and data and to develop efficient ways to integrate assessment and administrative databases.

Organizing Data

When recent technical advancements are coupled with the need to integrate diverse, disparate databases, the result is sometimes the creation of data warehouses and data marts. These repositories can provide an analytic environment that facilitates more efficient access to data needed for enrollment management purposes, as well as for other analysis and reporting needs. A wide array of current data and a more parsimonious array of historical data may often be available from such systems. Warehouses facilitate retrieval and analysis of data across different administrative systems and can provide linkages with ancillary databases. The primary pitfalls are the effort required to develop comprehensive warehouses and the administrative overhead needed to maintain them. Third party vendors have begun developing products to meet this need (Cold Fusion, for example).

Communicating Results

Effective enrollment management demands that information be shared with others regarding the recruitment, enrollment, retention, and graduation of students. Because students flow through institutions, how and when information is communicated is as important as what is communicated. Effective communication means getting the right information to the right people at the right time to do the right thing. In this section, six critical principles for placing enrollment management information in the hands of the decision-makers who need the information will be outlined.

The first principle of effective communication is knowing who needs the data. The organization of the institution may determine key decision makers who must have the information, but political considerations may determine who receives the information first. Every organization has a network of individuals who use the same information in different ways or need very different kinds of information for their specific decisions.

The second principle is knowing when the information is needed. If the right information is provided a day late, the decision will have been made without it. Being aware of when important decisions are being made on the campus is critical.

The third principle is knowing the best information reporting format and mode. Not only must the information processing style of the decision-maker be considered, but the mode by which it is delivered is an important consideration in designing the format. Traditionally, a print or text mode has been used for communicating information. While all findings should be documented in a written report to archive the information for historical reference, long and detailed reports are rarely read or used. Technology offers other options for sharing enrollment management information. Colleges and universities increasingly use the Internet for disseminating key information. Providing oral reports using computer-assisted presentation techniques is an excellent way to share information. This presentation mode provides the decision-makers an opportunity to query the presenter and pursue special topics related to the decision at hand. Questions can be raised and discussions initiated that may have implications for action.

The fourth principle is knowing how simply to communicate the research findings. The nature of the decision must be considered in light of the statistical sophistication of the user audience. Most decision-makers want to know what the reported data means and what implications it may have for the decision they are trying to make. That meaning should be communicated using simple numbers, percentages, and statistical averages (e.g., mean, median, or mode).

The fifth principle is knowing how formal the report should be. While a researcher may be asked to produce a long, formal, written report with extensive data analysis and strong recommendations for practice, it is more likely that a brief report, with a single table of data, one or two charts, and one or two recommendations for action, will be requested. In general, less is more. Too much data, and not enough information, merely frustrate decision-makers and interfere with the decision-making process.

The sixth principle is knowing how to deliver bad news to a decision-maker. If the information requested contains bad news, it may be helpful to release preliminary findings to key decision makers in time for them to develop a plan of action for dealing with the negative news. Few decision-makers want to look at a final draft or a formal report and be surprised by the findings, without having the opportunity to think of ways to consider the implications for dealing with the findings.

Communicating information is a process rather than a product. The researcher should search for ways to provide systematic institutional structures for sharing information with the right people, in the right format, at the right time.

Thinking of an information sharing process as providing their information rather than the researcher's information will make a huge improvement in getting decision-makers to use information.

THE FUTURE OF ENROLLMENT MANAGEMENT
Higher Education Trends

The future of enrollment management depends on the national higher education environment in which it will exist and to which it must respond. This environment might have the following characteristics:

- All national projections (WICHE, 1998; NCES, 1998; ETS, 2000) forecast sharp growth in higher education over the next 10-15 years as the baby boom echo (sometimes called "Generation Y") attends college

- Demographic changes will cause the South and West regions of the United States to have large enrollment increases while other areas experience smaller increases

- Hispanic and Asian enrollment will increase faster than the enrollment of other groups

- Funding for higher education will become increasingly competitive, complex, and, in many cases, scarce

- Accountability demands will continue to accelerate.

- Technology-delivered education, coupled with growing demands for wider access to academic programs, will blur geographic and educational sector boundaries.

Implications for Enrollment Management

Within this environment of higher education changes, enrollment management analysts may expect to observe several trends:

- **Enrollment management will become increasingly central to college and university missions**. Managing enrollments will become increasingly important as institutions compete for students in an environment where funding is often insecure. This will extend a trend that began for some institutions in the 1980s or even earlier. Researchers can expect to be asked for increased depth and breadth in their policy analyses. This might include better institutional data, multi-level analyses, more refined peer data, consideration of more issues, quicker response time, and dissemination to a wider audience.

- **Better integration with strategic planning and budgeting processes will occur**. Enrollment growth will become a more critical avenue for maintaining the revenue stream and developing discretionary funds for many institutions. Tuition increases and, in public institutions, the marginal revenue derived from state appropriations will forge stronger linkages with the budgeting and planning processes. Enrollment researchers will also need to be fiscal analysts.

- **The partnership between enrollment management and student assessment will strengthen**. As described in this chapter, assessment programs and enrollment management have a variety of common interests. As the assessment movement matures, enrollment researchers will increasingly integrate assessment data into their work, particularly with regard to student flow. Assessment studies and data will help understand how students move through the curriculum; they may also help institutions to design better recruitment strategies as faculty, staff and administrators get to know their students better.

- **Collaborations with other sectors and other institutions will increase**. Higher education boundaries are becoming less distinct. Technology-delivered education, dual enrollment of students in high school and community college courses, and baccalaureate degrees offered by community colleges are examples of initiatives that are changing the boundaries and increasing collaborative efforts across sectors and among institutions. The enrollment analyst will be working more with colleagues from other institutions as these complex issues are addressed.

References

Adelman, C. (1999) Answers in the toolbox: Academic intensity, attendance patterns and bachelor's degree attainment. Washington D.C.: U.S. Dept. of Education, Office of Educational Research and Improvement.

American College Testing Program (2000). Prediction service report. Available on the web at http://www.act.org/research/services/predict/index.html. Downloaded on November 28, 2000.

Andrade, S. J. (1999, May). Assessing the impact of curricular reform: Measures of course efficiency and effectiveness. Paper presented at the Annual Forum of the Association for Institutional Research, Seattle, WA.

Astin, A. W. (1993). What matters in college?: Four critical years revisited. San Francisco, CA: Jossey Bass.

Bauer, K. (1998). New Directions for Institutional Research: No. 98. Campus climate : Understanding the critical components of today's colleges and universities. San Francisco, CA: Jossey-Bass.

Brinkman, P. T., and McIntyre, C. (1997). New Directions for Institutional Research.:.No. 24. Methods and techniques of enrollment forecasting. (pp. 67-80).

Byers-Gonzalez, J. M. and DesJardins, S. L. (2001). *Artificial neural networks: A new approach for predicting application behavior.* Paper presented at the 2001 Association for Institutional Research Forum. Long Beach, CA.

Caldwell, R. (1999). Personal communication.

Clagett, C. A., and Kerr, H. S. (1992) An information infrastructure for enrollment management: Tracking and understanding your students. (ERIC Document Reproduction Service No. ED351075).

Cook, T. D., and Campbell, D. T. (1979). Quasi-experimentation: Design and analysis issues for field settings. Boston. MA : Houghton Mifflin.

Davis, J. S. (1997). Student aid research. A manual for financial aid administrators. Washington D.C.: National Association of Student Financial Aid Administrators.

Dennis, M. J. (1998). A practical guide to enrollment and retention management in higher education. Westport, CT: Greenwood Publishing Group.

DesJardins, S. L., Ahlburg, D. A., and McCall, B. P. (1999). *An event model of student departure.* Economics of Education Review, 18 (3), 375-90.

Dillman, D. A., (2000). Mail and internet surveys: The tailored design method (2nd ed.). New York, NY: Wiley.

Educational Testing Service (ETS). (2000). Crossing the great divide: Can we achieve equity when generation Y goes to college? Princeton, N.J.

Ewell, P. T. (1995). Working over time: The evolution of longitudinal student tracking data bases. New Directions for Institutional Research, 87, (pp. 7-19).

Fetterman, D. M. (Ed.). (1991). Using qualitative methods in institutional research. San Francisco, CA: Jossey-Bass

Hanson, G. R., and Swann, D. M. (1993). *Using multiple program impact analysis to document institutional effectiveness.* Research in Higher Education, 34 (1), (pp. 71-94).

Hanson, G. R., Norman, P., and Caillouet, C. (1998). *Conquering calculus: Intra-departmental variability in the efficiency and effectiveness of moving students through the math curriculum.* Paper presented at the 1998 AIR Forum. Seattle, WA.

Hathaway, R. S., (1995). *Assumptions underlying quantitative and qualitative research: Implications for institutional research.* Research in Higher Education, 36 (5).

Hossler, D., Bean, J. P., and Associates (1990). The strategic management of college enrollments. San Francisco, CA: Jossey-Bass.

Hossler, D., Schmitz, J., and Vespar, N. (1999). Going to college: How social, economic, and educational factors influence the decisions students make. Baltimore, MD: Johns Hopkins University Press.

House, E. R. (1980). Evaluating with validity. Beverly Hills, CA: Sage Publications.

Kemerer, F. R., Baldridge, V. J., & Green, K. C., (1982). Strategies for effective enrollment management. Washington, D.C.: American Association of State Colleges and Universities.

Kroc, R. J. and Hanson, G. R. (2001). *Enrollment management and student affairs.* Institutional research: Decision support in higher education. Tallahassee, FL: Association for Institutional Research

Kroc, R., Howard, R., Hull, P., and Woodard, D. (1997, May). Graduation rates: Do students' academic program choices make a difference? Paper presented at the Annual Forum of the Association for Institutional Research, Orlando, FL.

Mortenson, T. (1997, April). *Actual versus predicted institutional graduation rates for 1100 colleges and universities.* Post-Secondary Opportunity Newsletter. No. 58.

Morrison, J. L. (1992). *Welcome to volume one, number one!* On the Horizon, 1 (1).

National Center for Education Statistics (NCES). (1998). Pocket projections: Projections of education statistics to 2008. Washington, D.C.: U.S. Department of Education.

Seymour, E. and Hewitt, N. M. (1997). Talking about leaving: Why undergraduates leave the sciences. Boulder, CO: Westview Press.

Smith, T. Y., (Ed.). (1999). 1998-99 CSRDE report. University of Oklahoma: Center for Institutional Data Exchange and Analysis.

Suskie, L. A. (1992). Questionnaire survey research: What works (second edition). Tallahassee, FL: Association for Institutional Research.

Terenzini, P. T. (1993). *On the nature of institutional research and the knowledge and skills it requires.* Research in Higher Education, 34 (1), (pp. 1-10).

Tukey, J. W. (1977). Exploratory data analysis. Reading, MA: Addison-Wesley Publishing Company.

Voorhees, R. A. (1997). *Researching student aid: Creating an action agenda.* New Directions for Institutional Research, 24 (3), (pp. 99-107).

Western Interstate Commission for Higher Education (WICHE). (1998). Knocking at the college door—projections of high school graduates by state and ethnicity: 1996-2012. Boulder, CO

Chapter 6
Peer Institutions

Deborah J. Teeter, University of Kansas
Paul T. Brinkman, University of Utah

Introduction

Inter-institutional comparisons are often key factors in institutional strategic planning and decision-making. Comparative data provide managers with the ability to size up competition, provide benchmarks for assessing the well-being of their own institution, provide the ability to pinpoint areas deserving attention, and act as guides for policy development. Comparative data can also help explain and justify budget requests, salary increases, teaching loads, and tuition increases.

The success or failure of inter-institutional comparisons hinges upon the process of selecting peer institutions. This can be one of the most political processes with which the institutional researcher will have to deal.

In particular, to ensure that comparative data will serve the institution's intended purposes, the process of selecting comparison institutions is critical. The researcher needs to:

- Assess the overt and hidden political agendas surrounding the issues,

- Understand the various types of comparison groups that can be constructed, and

- Understand that the methodology used to select comparison institutions will, at some level, reflect the politics of the issue.

This chapter describes four types of comparison groups, as well as some methods for developing peers for an institution. The chapter also contains information about sources of data and other considerations in making comparisons.

Background

The literature on peer institutions fits roughly into one of two categories: the broader conceptual work on the uses of peer comparisons and discussions of methodology for selecting peers.

Chapters in several issues of *New Directions for Institutional Research* provide good overviews of the conceptual issues. The 1989 volume, "Enhancing Information Use in Decision-Making," provides broad discussions on the utilization of information, as well as suggested ways for communicating information to decision makers. The 1987 volume, "Conducting Interinstitutional Comparisons," includes chapters on sources of comparative data, methods for creating data sharing projects, use of comparative data, comparative financial analysis, and effective inter-institutional comparisons. The 1996 volume, "Inter-Institutional Data Exchange: When to Do It, What to Look for, and How to Make It Work," focuses on the benefits and hazards of participating in inter-institutional data exchanges. The appendix of this volume contains organizations and contacts for various exchanges. "Using Performance Indicators to Guide Strategic Decision Making," published in 1994, describes more than 250 potential performance indicators. The definition of institutional performance indicators may lead to an interest in comparative data on those indicators. The political considerations of exchanging and comparing data are presented in a chapter titled "The Politics of Comparing Data with Other Institutions" in an earlier 1983 volume.

The literature on structural methodologies for selecting peers starts with the 1981 work by Elsass and Lingenfelter. Their work is cited frequently as exemplifying the use of multivariate statistics, such as cluster analysis, in identifying peers. Subsequent literature details a number of approaches, including threshold and statistical models (Teeter & Christal, 1987) and clump analysis (McKeown & Moore, 1990).

Comparison Groups

Before beginning to select a comparison group, it is critical to understand the politics of using comparative data and to be knowledgeable about the various types of comparison groups. Then the most appropriate type of comparison group for the situation and purpose of the comparison can be determined.

Politics of Using Comparative Data

Because comparative data are often used to justify, explain, or advocate a certain position, it is important to understand how the intended audience, whether internal or external to the institution, looks upon comparative data. Organizational and political realities need to be considered and a strategy developed accordingly. If the audience is likely to be hostile to the idea of using comparative data, it is imperative to involve them early in the project. Concerns often center around the validity of the comparison group. If that is likely to be the case, the researcher should include the audience in the selection of the comparison institutions. Understanding the rationale and criteria used to select the comparison institutions may mitigate some of the audiences concerns. Obviously, the data the researcher draws upon should be accurate and easily understandable for the audience to properly assess the implications of the data.

The key to the successful use of comparative data is properly sizing up the environment in which the data are to be used and taking the steps necessary to ensure that the audience will be receptive. Failure to lay the groundwork may result in extensive delay or prohibit the use of comparative data.

Four Types of Comparison Groups

There are a number of different types of comparison groups. Each group can play a legitimate role in informing decision making, depending upon the situation. The issues to be addressed will influence the type of comparison group chosen. In earlier publications, four types of groups—competitor, aspirational, predetermined, and peer—were identified. These groups are displayed in Figure 1. Predetermined groups can be further differentiated as natural, traditional, jurisdictional, and classification-based.

A **competitor** group consists of institutions that compete with one another for students or faculty or financial resources. Although the institutions are competitors, they may not necessarily be similar in role and scope. For example, a shortage of faculty in a particular field, such as finance or accounting, may result in a four-year college competing with a university for the same faculty. Depending upon the purpose of the comparison, the lack of similarity may or may not be important.

Comparison, by definition, means examining both similarities and differences. Examining differences is critical in developing an **aspiration** group. An aspiration group includes institutions that are dissimilar to the home institution but worthy of emulation. When a comparison group contains numerous institutions that are clearly superior to the home institution, the group reflects aspiration more than commonality of mission.

The researcher should note that, if aspiration groups are presented as if they are peer groups, they can be costly in the political arena outside the campus. For example, if comparative data are used to buttress resource arguments, the masquerading of an aspiration group as a peer group may risk the credibility of most any comparative data the home institution wishes to use.

Figure 1 Four Types of Comparison Groups			
Competitor	Aspiration	Predetermined	Peer
		Natural Traditional Jurisdictional Classification-based	

It may fall to the institutional researcher to provide the reality check through assembling and presenting objective data on the alleged peers. If the appropriate data are chosen, the aspirational character of the proposed comparison group usually will be obvious. Still, individuals will ignore the obvious under certain circumstances, such as a no-holds-barred effort to increase funding. Therefore, the institutional researcher is advised to carefully assess where the comparative analysis fits in the overall institutional strategy. The task of moving comparative data into the decision-making process is often more important than the technical routines for working with comparative data.

A **predetermined** institutional comparison group consists of institutions arranged together for some purpose outside of the institution. A predetermined group falls into one of four general categories: natural, traditional, jurisdictional, and classification-based.

Natural groups are those that are based on one or more of the following types of relationships: membership in an athletic conference, membership in a regional compact or location in a region of the country. In effect, institutions already belong to a highly visible grouping of some sort; therefore, it is natural to think of them as being comparable. They may indeed be comparable in some inherent sense, but the nature of the specific comparison is the critical test.

A *traditional* comparison group is one that is based on history. It has the advantage of being familiar and may enjoy wide acceptance. However, it may or may not be an appropriate comparison in a given situation.

A *jurisdictional* group consists of institutions that are compared simply because they are part of the same political or legal jurisdiction. Frequently, the boundary for this type of group is the state line. Not surprisingly, elected officials and state agency staff will make comparisons of institutions within their purview, even though the institutions may have little else in common. Once again, the comparison issue in question should be the primary factor in determining the appropriateness of this kind of comparison group.

A *classification-based* group is one used for national reporting. Probably the best known is the classification developed by the Carnegie Commission in the 1970s, periodically updated, then further modified in 2000 (http://www.carnegiefoundation.org/classification/classification.htm).

The American Association of University Professors (AAUP) uses an institutional classification for reporting comparative faculty salaries (see the annual March-April issue of *Academe*).

Using a classification-based comparison group saves time and effort. Further, the classifications have credibility and name recognition. The problem with the ready-made groups is that they typically are based on only a few comparative dimensions, such as size and the extent of research activity. As a result, they may contain too much within-group variation for certain types of comparative analysis.

A **peer** group consists of institutions that are similar in role, scope and/or mission. In this case, *similar* rather than *identical* is the operative word. It is unrealistic to expect to find clones of the home institution, unless the criteria for comparison are limited to categorical variables such as "public, land-grant, located west of the Mississippi." When interval variables are used to describe size, program content or amount of research, it is unlikely that a perfect match between any two institutions will be found. However, *similar* institutions usually can be identified.

Developing a Peer Group

There are a number of procedures for developing peer groups. Options range from statistical approaches to those that depend entirely on judgment. **Figure 2** describes the typology of the most popular procedures. The top half of **Figure 2** describes the continuum of options and the bottom half indicates the techniques themselves (the techniques are meant to be a representative, rather than an exhaustive, list). In this chapter, each of the techniques will be briefly described in terms of the continuum, then an example of a procedure will be provided.

Cluster analysis and supporting factor-analytic and discriminant techniques are characterized by heavy reliance on multivariate statistics and computer processing. An advantage of cluster analysis is that a large number of institutional descriptors can readily be handled. These statistical techniques tend to de-emphasize the judgment of administrator input. The hybrid approach incorporates a strong emphasis on data and on input from administrators, combined with statistical algorithms for manipulating data. The threshold approach also emphasizes a formal, systematic approach to data and to administrator input; however it depends little, if at all, on statistical algorithms. In the panel approach, administrator input is heavily emphasized; some data may be included informally but not systematically or comprehensively.

Figure 2
A Typology of Procedures for Developing Peer Groups

Emphasis			
Data & Statistics	Data & Statistics & Judgment	Data & Judgment	Judgment
Cluster Analysis	Hybrid Approach	Threshold Approach	Panel Review
Technique			

Threshold Approach

Various types of threshold procedures are available. One example is the approach developed and used by the National Center for Higher Education Management Systems (NCHEMS). The NCHEMS procedure combines raw data, thresholds, weights, and a modest statistical algorithm. The process utilizes both nominal variables, such as public versus private control, and interval variables, such as enrollment and the number of degree programs.

In the typical application, the nominal variables are used to reduce the universe of relevant institutions. For example, if "public control" is considered an essential characteristic for a potential peer institution, then any institution not publicly controlled is eliminated from further consideration.

After the nominal variables have been used to generate a subset of institutions, the interval variables are used to rank order the remaining institutions. Points are assigned to each institution, based on the importance attached to each interval variable and the number of times an institution misses a prescribed range. Each miss on an important variable pushes the candidate institution down the list, further away from the home institution. The points are the basis for a rank order. The rank-ordered list is meant to be a guide for analysts and administrators at the home institution, who make the final selection of institutions for their comparison group.

Table 1 displays a list of characteristics typically used by NCHEMS when selecting peers for four-year colleges and universities. The nominal variables (Part 1) are used to eliminate any candidate institution that does not meet the criteria checked (contact NCHEMS for the specifics regarding the tables that are referenced in Part 1). The interval variables (Part 2) are used to move institutions up or down a list of possible comparison institutions. Ranges are established by the home institution; the frequency with which an institution falls outside of the home institution's ranges will place it further down the list. Additionally, a weighted score is calculated using the importance scale. A miss counts one point if the variable is "very important," one-half point for "important," and no points for an unimportant variable. The weighted sum is used to rank order the candidate institutions. Therefore, an institution's rank on a list of comparisons is a function of how well it fits the criteria and the weights assigned to those criteria. Based on the criteria established, a list of institutions is rank ordered by their "closeness" to the home institution.

Although the threshold approach provides an ordered guide, the selection of comparison criteria, weights, and ranges, as well as the final selection of peers, are all dependent upon the expert judgment of analysts and administrators. The procedure is designed to channel and highlight judgment based on the data. The transparency of the procedure is a strength but it also can be a vehicle for manipulation. Manipulation can be countered only by designing appropriate checks and balances into the overall process of selecting a comparison group.

Data

All the models for selecting comparison institutions require data. There are several ways in which comparative data can be acquired:
- Using *national databases*,
- Joining a formal *data exchange* group that exists for the mutual benefit of participating parties, and
- Collecting data on an *ad hoc* basis from selected institutions.

National Databases

There are a number of national databases that can be used to acquire data for selecting comparison groups. For example, the opening web page of the Integrated Postsecondary Education Data System (IPEDS) Peer Analysis System states that "it is a tool designed to enable a user to easily compare a postsecondary institution of the user's choice to a group of peer institutions, also selected by the user. This is done by generating reports using selected IPEDS variables of interest" (http://nces.ed.gov/ipedspas/ updated November 29, 2000). This tool is particularly valuable for acquiring IPEDS data for a set of

Table 1
NCHEMS Information Services
Comparison Group Selection Service

Contact Name:
Address:

Target Institution:

Part 1: Selection Criteria	
Items	**Check here to use as a Selection Criteria and Indicate additional Codes to include in Selection Criteria**
Control (Public/Private, Nonprofit/Private, For Profit)	
Land-grant Institution (Yes/No)	
Medical school (Yes/No)	
City Size (See Table)	
Region (See Table)	
Carnegie Classification (See Table)	

Carnegie Classification (See Table)					
			Importance Level (Check One)		
Weighting Criteria Items	**Target Institution**	**Range**	**Very**	**Somewhat**	**Not**
Total FTE Students					
Total Headcount					
% Part-time Headcount					
% Minority Headcount					
Full-time Faculty Headcount					
% Certificates					
% Associates					
% Bachelors					
% Masters					
% Doctorates					
% First Professional					
Certificate Programs					
Associate Programs					
Bachelor's Programs					
Master's Programs					
Doctoral Programs					
First Professional Programs					
% Academic Degrees - 4 Year					
% Natural Science Degrees - 4 Year					
% Social Science Degrees - 4 Year					
% Humanities Degrees - 4 Year					
% Health Science Degrees - 4 Year					
% Engineering Degrees - 4 Year					
% Business Degrees - 4 Year					
% Education Degrees - 4 Year					
% Computer Degrees - 4 Year					
% Arts and Science Awards - 2 Year					
% Health Awards - 2 Year					
% Bus and Data Proc. Awards - 2 Year					
% Service Awards - 2 Year					
% Trade Awards - 2 Year					
% Technical Awards - 2 Year					
Research/Instruction Expenditures Ratio					
Total Research Expenditures					

For questions, please call (303) 497-0314
All data provided by NCHEMS are from IPEDS files.

Note: Please include a range for every weighting criteria item that you have marked as very or somewhat important.

institutions. The user may select institutions by name (e.g., a predetermined natural group such as an athletic conference) or identify potential peer institutions using variables and ranges of data values that are similar to a target institution. The data from this system can always feed into more sophisticated models for selecting peers.

ANSWERS (Accessing National Surveys with Electronic Research Sources) is hosted by the National Center for Education Statistics (NCES) (http:/ /nces.ed.gov/npec/answers/). It provides "a guide or portal to information about national datasets at the postsecondary institution level." The ANSWERS project was funded by the National Postsecondary Cooperative (NPEC) which was authorized by Congress in 1994 to promote "comparable and uniform information and data at the federal, state, and institutional levels." NPEC is sponsored by NCES.

WebCASPAR, hosted by the National Science Foundation (NSF) (http:// caspar.nsf.gov/webcaspar), is a database system that provides "quick and convenient access to a wide range of data on academic resources." Users can select specific data, review them on screen, and output them to a file. Data in WebCASPAR are derived from numerous surveys sponsored by the NSF and NCES, as well as other sources.

Data Exchanges

There are a number of formal data exchanges in higher education. They may serve as sources of comparative data for use in a public context, if the policies and practices of the exchanges permit such usage.

The formal data exchanges typically make possible the sharing of more detailed and timely information than can be gained from public sources. Joint development of data formats, data definitions, and exchange procedures enhance the comparability of the shared data. Data exchange networks also have the advantage of reducing the number of redundant requests for data among institutions that are interested in the same type of comparative data. In addition, routine exchange through networks helps build longitudinal data for trend analysis. Formal exchanges often incorporate explicit guidelines for the use and sharing of the data, providing some assurance to participating institutions on the handling of their data.

Ad Hoc Collection

The collection of data on an ad hoc basis is probably the least desirable method. The time and effort needed for extensive data collection may very well exceed the value of the data collected. One issue is the difficulty in assuring comparability of ad hoc data. In addition, it is often difficult to motivate institutions to provide extensive information when the effort does not have tangible and immediate rewards. The exchange of ad hoc data for a particular issue may be viable, but it is not a good way to collect the kind of data typically used to select peers or other kinds of comparison institutions.

Limitations

The fundamental data concerns of validity, accuracy, and reliability are always present within a comparative context. Establishing how well these concerns are met is often more challenging when doing comparative analysis, because comparative data are often derived from multiple sources. Also, the rules and definitions for recording such data may be inconsistent across sources. The close familiarity that can be so helpful in spotting data errors is usually missing because one typically must depend on secondary sources.

The use and purpose of the comparison determines, in part, the extent to which errors of a given kind may compromise the comparison. For example, management-control situations may require highly accurate data; whereas, data that are to be used in a strategic-planning context probably could be less accurate, in the sense of being precise, without causing problems.

Remember

Institutional comparisons are best begun exactly where any good analysis begins: with a clear sense of purpose. Once the purpose has been determined, the researcher can address the technical and the human/political dimensions of the comparison process.

Both the technical and the human/political dimensions are important. On the technical side, the main area of concern is data. The act of comparing data from other institutions with the home institution compounds the typical data concerns of validity, accuracy, and reliability. The best approach is to proceed with caution, assuming as little as possible about the quality of the data. On the human/political side, although there are a number of procedures available for selecting comparison groups, the researcher should choose one that suits the researcher's analytic skills, the purpose of the comparison, and the broader political aspects of the task. To get by politically, the procedure chosen must appear reasonable and valid to those who are to use its results. Involving interested parties in the process often helps, especially if the involvement is well managed and occurs early in the process, when the purpose of the comparison is being specified and the selection criteria are being developed.

Even a solid analytic approach to selecting peer institutions, in which the data and the selection methodology are carefully and thoughtfully chosen, is no guarantee of success. Funding levels and institutional prestige, two of the most important issues for most colleges and universities, are often directly or indirectly affected by the development of peer groups. Thus, analytical considerations are sometimes swamped by intense political struggles. This is especially likely to occur in the public sector, where funding, and perhaps even prestige, can sometimes be a zero-sum game.

In spite of the political struggles, the selection of comparison institutions, and the use of comparative data, continues.

References

Borden, V. M. H. & Banta, T. W. (Eds.). (1994) <u>New Directions for Institutional Research: No. 82. Using performance indicators to guide strategic decision making</u>. San Francisco, CA: Jossey-Bass.

Brinkman, P. T. (Ed.). (1987). <u>New Directions for Institutional Research: No. 53. Conducting interinstitutional comparisons</u>. San Francisco, CA: Jossey-Bass.

Elsass, J. E., and Lingerfelter, P. E. (1981). *An identification of college and university peer groups.* Illinois Board of Higher Education, 500 Reisch Building, 4 West Old Capital Square, Springfield, IL 62701.

Ewell, P.E. (Ed.). (1989). <u>New Directions for Institutional Research: No. 64. Enhancing information use in decision-making</u>. San Francisco, CA: Jossey-Bass.

McKeown, M. P., & Moore, N. (1990). *A new method for selecting peer institutions.* Paper presented at the annual meeting of the Rocky Mountain Association for Institutional Research, Missoula, MT.

Teeter, D. J. (1983). *The politics of comparing data with other institutions.* In J. W. Firnberg & W. F. Lasher (Eds.), <u>New Directions for Institutional Research: No. 38. The politics and pragmatics of institutional research</u>. San Francisco, CA: Jossey-Bass. (pp. 39-48).

Teeter, D. J., & Christal, M. E. (1987). *Establishing peer groups: A comparison of methodologies.* <u>Planning for Higher Education,</u> *15* (2), (pp. 8-17).

Trainer, J. (1996). <u>New Directions for Institutional Research: No. 89. Inter-institutional data exchange: When to do it, what to look for, and how to make it work</u>. San Francisco, CA: Jossey-Bass.

Additional Resources

Della Mea, C. L. (1989). *A comparison of two procedures for peer group assignment of institutions of higher education* (Doctoral dissertation, Virginia Polytechnic Institute and State University, Blacksburg, VA). Publication #8915719, University Microfilms, Inc., 1490 Eisenhower Place, P.O. Box 975, Ann Harbor, MI 48104.

Parker, R. G. (1992). *My institution has no peers.* Paper presented at the annual meeting of the Rocky Mountain Association for Institutional Research, Couer D'Alene, Idaho.

Weeks, S. F., Puckett, D., and Daron R. (2000). *Developing peer groups for the Oregon University System: From politics to analysis (and back).* Research in Higher Education, 41 (1), (pp. 1-20).

Zhao, J. and Dean, D. C. (1997, May). *Selecting peer institutions: A hybrid approach.* Paper presented at the Thirty-Seventh Annual Forum of the Association for Institutional Research, Orlando, FL. (Eric Document Reproduction Service No. ED410877.)

Chapter 7
Using the Web for Institutional Research

Tod Massa
Virginia State Council of Higher Education

Introduction

This chapter could describe Web sites and data sources that can be used for institutional research (IR). Simulations of data collection and information lookup could also be included. In each case, part of what would be written would likely be out of date by publication. Instead, this chapter approaches the enterprise of Web-enabled institutional research from a theoretical perspective of institutional research and knowledge management (KM).

In recent years, higher education has tended to treat the Web as a vast, unedited library, existing without a rational collection policy. While this model is not necessarily wrong, it is perhaps more useful to view the Web as a living organism. After all, the Web does seem to grow and behave rather organically. The only controls on the Web are those imposed from without, much like the effect of using asphalt and concrete to create pathways, or, in some instances, using weed-killer to kill growth in spots unintended for such growth.

Every day, new Web sites are established and other Web sites disappear; the Web is a dynamic environment. Not only do sites come and go, but the information on those sites is transient as well. Web pages are designed with dynamic content that may update predictably, or not so predictably, depending on the design. Sites such as the Chronicle of Higher Education (http://www.chronicle.com) and CNN (http://www.cnn.com) update daily. In fact, CNN updates its site throughout the day with breaking news.

Some sites enhance the user experience by e-mailing registered users when the site changes and new material is posted. Other sites "push" the material directly to subscribers when content changes by encoding a "refresh" command within the page. (The PGA Tour site http://www.pgatour.com does this with tournament scores on a cycle of about once a minute.) In 1997, a long time ago in Internet-time (an expression used to denote the rapid pace of change on the Internet), Jesse Berst, in his ZDNet editorial (http://www5.zdnet.com/anchordesk/story/story_761.html) announced the death of the Web browser in favor of push technology (as opposed to the pull technology of traditional browsing). However, in examining the current crop of browsers and the Web sites available, it is clear that push technology has not taken over. While it is alive and well, so is the original pull technology.

As any institutional researcher or other "knowledge worker" can readily attest, particularly anyone who has the opportunity to closely observe executives at work, the amount of information that people receive on a daily basis is virtually obscene. It is often too much to process easily. Self-help books and executive success books are full of ways to manage daily information flow. E-mail

114

applications allow users to create processing rules to direct incoming messages to specified folders. This includes the option to automatically delete unwanted messages. When one receives hundreds of messages a day, this feature is an obvious improvement over sorting and filing each bit of incoming mail. Push technology, while eliminating the need to look for desired information, most often includes excess information of little or no value to the user, thus requiring more filtering by the user. Ultimately, both forms of filtering are imperfect but can lead to greater effectiveness in information processing.

Managing information flow today is akin to taking a drink of water from a fire hose. Using the Web for institutional research is somewhat less of a challenge; however, it requires many of the same strategies that it takes to keep from drowning when drinking from the fire hose of today's information stream. This chapter will focus on three major conceptual issues: the Web as an organic medium, connective sense-making, and applying the Web to the institutional research life-cycle. And, finally we will take a look to the future.

The Organic Web

The concept of the Web as an organic medium has already been introduced. However, there has not yet been a discussion regarding the implications for institutional research under this model of the Web.

A Web site appears. There may or may not be a pushed announcement such as an e-mail. In the absence of an announcement, how does a researcher become aware of the site, much less make a prima facie evaluation of its utility? Knowledge of the site may be acquired through incidental experience or given to the researcher directly by another party. The modern-day knowledge worker does not know that a new site has come into existence, unless some type of action is taken. For example, on a regular basis, the knowledge worker can execute a variety of manual searches to locate new sites within the criteria specified. The researcher may opt to employ the use of software agents like WebFerret, to conduct these searches automatically, then be notified when new sites are discovered.

To be useful, knowledge regarding Web sites needs to be organized, perhaps categorized with descriptions detailing the type, or format, of the data they contain. After collecting the data, organizing it into meaning is the next step on the road to developing a networked intelligence. The goal in organizing data is, usually, to create a system that is intuitive and logical. However, what the creator finds logical and intuitive may not be so to other people. Thus, many large organizations have developed protocols for filing. For example, the United States Army devotes an entire manual to creating a standard filing system allowing anyone from one installation to readily access the files at another installation.

This need for organization leads naturally into a discussion of standards. In light of the concept of the Army's filing system, it might appear that standards are what lead to a shared intelligence. It is not the standards, but the process of organization, that really creates intelligence. The use of standards, however, makes the intelligence shareable or, at least, interpretable.

Real intelligence comes from the organizing and processing of information, not just its collection. It also comes from the associations made along the way as described in the following section.

Connective Sense-Making

Connections between synapses in the brain are the key to the storage of knowledge. Similarly, connections between Web sites and other knowledge are what create networked intelligence. These connections are created not only in the mind of the user, but in the way the links, shortcuts and references are stored as well as how individual pages are linked to one another. It is possible that these links might be more important than the information on the individual pages. Linkage between pages give meaning that wasn't there before. For example, http://research.schev.edu/enrollment/E2_Report.asp "SCHEV Research Enrollment Report E2" is a Web page providing Fall semester headcount enrollments by institution, in a variety of cross tabulations. By itself, it tells little beyond the facts of enrollment. Likewise, http://research.schev.edu/fair/tag2_report.asp "SCHEV Research Tuition Assistance Grant (TAG) Summary" provides a record of the number of recipients and total awards of Virginia's Tuition Assistant Grant (TAG) to students at private institutions for Fall and Spring semesters. By combining the statistics provided on these two pages, a researcher can easily determine the proportion of students at a given private college that receive TAG. That is only a start though. By linking to other parts of the State Council of Higher Education for Virginia (SCHEV) Web site or the Virginia General Assembly site, one can learn that TAG is only for Virginia residents (those meeting domicile requirements for example): http://leg1.state.va.us/cgi-bin/legp504.exe?021+ful+HB475) after further research/linking, a researcher can also find various parts of the Code of Virginia that build a legislative history of TAG. Working back the other direction, a researcher can focus on an individual institution and link to its Web site, in order to develop a context for the type of students receiving TAG.

By including these connections as links in a word-processing document surrounded by text providing the necessary context, illumination and discussion, one can create a powerful means of effective communication. This is different from the traditional research paper only to the extent that the actual data and information accumulated from the Web are not dynamically accessed from the document itself.

Dynamism and connectedness are what make the Web what it is. The Web has the ability to link to data that are updated regularly and pass the links to those data along with the document. Ultimately, the data from those connections are available from just about any Internet-connected computer.

This type of transformation is the power of the Web. Any user can access any public Web site, as long as they have the technology and the connection. The document containing the links provides the context that anchors everything

116

together; it creates information power that can be shared, making it more useful. Even, or perhaps most especially, when the data or Web sites are not publicly accessible, the power is multiplied or, at the very least, focused. This technology enables a user, even one with minimal skill, to have access to large stores of knowledge. For users possessing greater skills in authoring, in creating assemblages of information, so much more is possible.

The current model discussed in this chapter relies on the reader of the document to follow the link(s), working in the same manner as footnotes or appendices. Using IFRAMES (an independent, floating frame element), a researcher can actually embed the content of the link, driving the user to observe the content. Microsoft Windows Object Linking and Embedding (OLE) technology promises that a user can build a complex object created from documents from other locations and other applications. Such capabilities allow the user to embed a spreadsheet as a dynamic object that can be edited, always reflecting the most current data. Using IFRAMES, Web documents become complex devices for conveying data, meaning, context, and knowledge.

Data leads to information; information and context lead to knowledge; knowledge, experience and judgment lead to wisdom. As useful as technology allowing users to link and combine Web pages is, it still only answers part of the primary question of "How to use the Web for institutional research?"

Applying the Web to the Institutional Research Life-Cycle

Institutional research is undeniably a data-driven profession. Regardless of where the practitioner falls within the matrix developed by Borden, Massa, and Milam (2001), the practitioner of institutional research works in the arena of converting data to information. Thus, the next logical question becomes how to use the Web most effectively to convert data to information.

The life cycle of institutional research described by Borden, Massa, and Milam (2001), divided into five segments: design, collection, preparation, analysis, and dissemination (publication). Any of these segments alone could be the focus of Web-based institutional research. Previously, a generic conglomeration of these tasks to create an electronic publication with the appropriate links has been discussed. In this section, each segment will be investigated separately to create an understanding of how the Web can be used to enhance the activity in each segment.

Design

The design of an institutional research project sets the context for the research. Ultimately, the design provides the meaning of the research, determining to a large extent the validity of the effort. The Web plays a role by providing a platform to determine if there are existing project designs with goals similar to the goals of a planned project. For example, the Web can be used as a communication medium to share ideas more actively, through such means as solicitation of assistance through newsletters (like the *Electronic AIR*) or through telecommunication options such as video conferencing. There also are many

117

online journals and other forms of discipline-specific resources that can be of great utility to the social science-type research upon which institutional research is based. In short, the Web serves as a ready resource to find what has already been done.

Collection

Today, data acquisition via the Web is easier than ever. In fact, data acquisition, in general, is easier than ever. From the National Center for Education Statistics' (NCES) Web site (http://nces.ed.gov/ipeds), a researcher can access the IPEDS Peer Analysis Tool and download a wide range of the IPEDS data available for a selected group of institutions or download an entire survey collection. Additionally, calculated variables integrated into the tables of data can also be created. Researchers may use the National Science Foundation (NSF) Web site and download data from WebCaspar and NSF-specific surveys into a variety of formats. Both of these federal government sites have multiple levels of access available, including anonymous access, that provide more interesting, or more recent, data.

One of the challenges to using national datasets is knowing where to find them. Fortunately, there is an excellent resource, ANSWERS (Accessing National Surveys with Electronic Research Sources) (http://nces.ed.gov/npec/answers). ANSWERS provides researchers access to the topics and variables of a range of national surveys. It is a tremendous resource for researchers that do not know where to find needed data.

At the state level, the SHEEOs (State Higher Education Executive Officers – http://www.sheeo.org for a list of the relevant Web sites) provide a range of data products, from IPEDS-type data to cross-tabulations that are specific to the interests of that particular state. The California SHEEO, for example, has a data system that works on the principle of a Microsoft Wizard, requiring the user to respond to a single question or option at a time to build the data request and resultant display. Some SHEEO sites provide specific performance measures or tools to perform Web-based policy analysis such as dynamic reports with live graphing. On-Line Analytical Processing (OLAP) cubes that are essentially pivot tables (used by many in Microsoft Excel) based on millions of rows of data, instead of mere thousands, are under development at a small number of SHEEOs. The Virginia SHEEO site has such a Web site. Other state Web sites may include key indicator data that provide metrics of institutional performance on statewide policy goals, such as the Kentucky SHEEO.

Some institutions' institutional research offices publish a variety of usable data on the Web. George Mason University in Virginia was an early adopter of the Web-based data-warehousing concept. It hosts a very usable site, at http://irr.gmu.edu/institutiondata.cfm providing data on key indicators or building and room usage, complete with drill-downs and rollups. These sites, while useful, can often be hard to find.

Some of the most interesting data can be found at the *US News and World Report America's Best Colleges* Web site (http://www.usnews.com/usnews/edu/

college/rankings/). Unfortunately, these data are not easily downloadable and the data often are grouped into different pages. However, if a researcher looks at the URL "At a glance" page for his or her own institution, it is readily observed that the institution's FICE code is part of the URL. Therefore, by collecting the FICE codes of the schools for which the researcher wishes to collect data (*i.e.*, a peer group), the desired page where the data of interest lie can be selected. The data may then be entered into a spreadsheet or database. Then simply replace the four- or five-digit number in the URL for the next institution's FICE code in the list. For example, change the 10448 in http://www.usnews.com/usnews/edu/college/directory/drfinaid_10448.htm to 3227 hit the Enter key and when the page reloads it displays Willamette University's data instead of data for Thomas Aquinas College. This short cut is a simple, but effective, trick of the allowing rapid acquisition of data.

Preparation

Once the data has been collected, preparation of the data for research is probably the step least amenable to the benefits of the Web. There are ways, however to harness the Web for this task. For instance, a researcher can use the Web to validate data already collected. Perhaps of more value, and more readily performed, is the ability to locate documents (such as the NCES publications "The Student Data Handbook" and "The Staff Data Handbook") in order to apply standards of formatting, definitions, and valid value tables to the project.

Analysis

Typically, when pondering the analysis phase of the basic institutional research project, a researcher thinks about the software used for the analysis or the specific methodologies applied. However, analysis also consists of such actions as triangulation and result validation. The results of the analysis can be compared to existing results previously published and available on the Web. The Web also contains resources for interpreting statistical results; some are useful, some are not. Effective use of the Web during the analysis phase can also help the researcher understand the context of the data or the events under examination.

From a strictly technical perspective, the Web is a blessing during this phase because it allows the researcher to acquire much needed software updates and patches. Undoubtedly, the most useful aspect of the Web during analysis is the possibility for interaction with colleagues to discuss possible interpretations of the results. E-mail, Microsoft NetMeeting and other teleconferencing options (including AOL Instant Messenger and other chat applications) provide immediate avenues for communication. The use of conferencing and collaboration software allows users on opposite coasts of a continent, or across continents, not only to discuss the results, and to share the data and applications while using a shared electronic whiteboard on the researchers' computer, much like a traditional whiteboard in a conference room. These are powerful tools for analysis.

Dissemination

Dissemination, or publication, is the other phase in which the Web shines as a vehicle for institutional research. Regardless of the size of the dataset or the results, the Web is a nearly ideal medium for publication. From a single page of results, as in an executive summary, down to the source data itself, the information can be published and interlinked within itself, allowing the reader to drill up or down between levels of aggregation of the data as desired. The reader can also link to external sites to provide comparisons, national or local context, or simply to view references used in the literature review or just about anything on the Web with relative ease. The tools have evolved, and continue to evolve, to a point where Web publication is no longer a secondary or optional function; it is becoming a primary function, or at least a primary expectation, of many users.

The technology of Web-focused publication has changed dramatically. However, technology and institutional image control issues still create problems. The technological problems arise from the many multiple methods of publication and different technologies available. For example, the primary institutional Web-servers often use Unix or Linux operating systems. These systems are maintained by central administrative computing. These systems are not as amenable to the Web publishing features of Microsoft products that are installed on most desktops.

This does not mean that there are not extraordinary tools for these systems, there are. There are also very good tools that are free, such as PHP and MySQL. Unfortunately, it may be more of a question of finding support and local training to use these tools, especially if the researcher chooses to focus on using a database on the back-end to drive the data-delivery of the Web site. Fortunately, these are not insurmountable issues. Some institutional research offices are able to invest in their own dedicated Web-servers, thus determining what operating systems and support applications they use. This ability requires developing new skill sets for most institutional researchers that may not be possible given current levels of demand for institutional research products and other drains on the researcher's time.

Ultimately, these choices are matters of preference and require the balancing of resources in order for the institutional research office or practitioner to determine what alternatives to choose. The practitioner should select the options that best fit the specific situation, including the authoring and programming skills of the potential Web author/developer or the availability of training.

It is important for the researcher to understand that there are security issues with any and all of the hardware/software platforms and all the applications. Despite the hype and the prevalent anti-Microsoft attitudes, Unix and Linux both have to be maintained constantly. Software patches are made available weekly, sometimes even daily, for these systems. Any server exposed to the outside world of the Internet needs that kind of attention to remain secure. In other words, no system is so stable that it does not require regular maintenance and near-constant attention. If the institutional research office is not prepared to apply this level of care and nurturing to maintaining a server, then it is best to use established institutional servers or, at least, negotiate the care and maintenance with the institution's information technology department.

In summary, there is a great deal of potential for applying the Web to the life cycle of institutional research. There is not a phase of the institutional research life cycle where the Web cannot be beneficial. The Web provides new avenues of communication and publication that can reach widely around the world.

The Future...and Unused Bits of the Present

Previously, this chapter has directed researchers struggling with the notion of Web-focused publication or merely delivering Adobe PDF files, or simple HTML-exported files, with no connectivity to other pages. But what lies beyond? For those that carry Palm Pilots, PocketPCs or similar hand-held devices, services, such as AvantGo (http://www.avantgo.com/), provide automatic synchronization and downloads with the current news and events. This can be ideal for hip-pocket environmental scanning, for example, reading targeted news while on the bus or waiting for a meeting to start. It is extremely easy to develop a "channel" of Web content, which changes dynamically throughout the day and pushes performance measures and other critical information to administrators.

In the realm of hand-held computing, exciting database possibilities have become available. Using Microsoft SQL Server, a researcher can develop databases for the PocketPC. (The PocketPC uses a Microsoft Windows variant for its operating system.) Such databases can provide ready access to various institutional research data with relative ease. These data can be updated through synchronization by direct connection to a desktop computer, traditional telephone modem dial-up, or wireless networking.

Wireless networking with such handheld devices truly opens up a world with information at the researcher's fingertips. A researcher could be in a high-level meeting, or testifying in a legislative committee, and be able to respond immediately to a question that had not been anticipated. It's a marvelous use of technology and institutional research. The only downsides to wireless networking are the lack of widespread high-speed, wireless networks and the need to create data pages in a format that is somewhat less rich than what is available in full-featured Web pages.

The Web has been discussed in this chapter as a set of interesting technologies. However, a time is rapidly approaching, though, when the Web will be much more than that; the technologies supporting the Web will be more incidental than anything else. Today, the Web is part of core business activities in higher education; it will continue that role well into the future. Yet, the Web still has not met its potential to be the single most important communication medium in the world. Once the evolutionary nature of the Web and its technologies have slowed, then the technologies of the Web will become incidental. The work of institutional researchers will then be automatically, and seamlessly, published according to a basic set of established rules. The time to start learning the Web and studying its implications for institutional research is now.

References

Borden, V., Massa, T., and Milam, J. (2001). *Technology and tools for institutional research.* In R. D. Howard (Ed.), Institutional research: Decision support in higher education. Tallahassee, FL: Association for Institutional Research. (pp. 195-222).

Chapter 8
Using National Datasets for
Postsecondary Education Research

John H. Milam, Jr.
HigherEd.org, Inc.

Introduction

With the ubiquitous World Wide Web, there is unprecedented, free access to a growing number of valuable datasets about postsecondary education. Almost every federal and state agency, association, and education-related organization has been forced to justify its existence and rethink its programs by making its data collections more readily accessible and meaningful to its constituents. This is a consequence, in part, of the fact that there have never been more data collected, whether mandated or voluntarily, in print and online. This process was once a very costly enterprise of survey design, sampling, mailing, scanning, data entry, analysis, adjudication, publication, and marketing. However, Web-enabled data access has transformed the collection and dissemination of all types of postsecondary information. Complex annual data collections, such as the Integrated Postsecondary Education Data Systems (IPEDS), that took several years to be released and published are now available on the Web just weeks after they close.

While learning to use these datasets, users should not be discouraged by the sheer complexity and number. The online tools for creating extracts and for analysis have never been easier to use and are undergoing dramatic improvements in meeting user needs. However, this chapter is simply a starting point in the process; and researchers should carefully explore the range of online resources that are documented.

Once obtained, the skills needed to explore any one dataset and find patterns in data are easily translated into working with the data dictionaries and the methodological concerns of others. Regardless of the dataset, users need to understand data elements and how they are defined. Users need to ask how the data can be meaningfully queried, grouped, sorted, aggregated, graphed, displayed, analyzed, and reported. And most importantly, users must know the data integrity of a dataset.

The first section of this chapter focuses on a review of the different ways to approach locating datasets. The discussion will be limited to large data collections which may be used for a variety of purposes and include a large sample size. The major data collections of the federal government will be reviewed in depth in section two, along with some widely recognized surveys by national postsecondary education associations and commercial vendors. After finding out about a dataset, a researcher must understand how to access it, which is addressed in section three. Once users begin to explore a data source in depth, there are other questions which must be addressed, which are documented in section four. A brief review of emerging trends in data collection and references follow. This chapter closely parallels the work of the author in directing a project for the National Postsecondary Education Cooperative (NPEC) funded by the United States Department of Education's National Center for Education Statistics (NCES), called ANSWERS. ANSWERS is a Web site with a set of online tools for "Accessing National Surveys with Electronic Research Sources" (http://nces.ed.gov/npec/answers).

ANSWERS tools include a matrix of variables from national surveys, a question bank from the national sample surveys, a definition bank, references regarding survey development and using the national datasets, an inventory of national surveys, information about survey developers, a list of datasets with information about variables, and a list of subjects/topical areas by dataset. Special audience pages are designed to offer help in finding data to associations, federal agencies, state agencies, institutional researchers and planners, policy analysts, survey developers, and the media.

Figure 1
Screen capture of ANSWERS Web Site

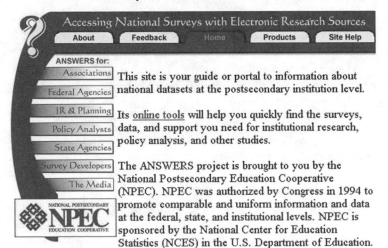

Using Different Lenses for Finding Data

In conducting institutional research, there are different approaches or lenses to use in finding needed data: topical, source, level of aggregation, collection method, time/date, and desired manipulation of the data.

The most obvious of these approaches is *topical*, in which the researcher looks for data by broad subject (*i.e.*, faculty, students, or financial aid)   The search is then narrowed (*i.e.*, faculty rank or tenure status). The researcher must have knowledge of specific datasets and/or access to tools that will assist in quickly finding the data needed by topic. One example of these tools is the

Table 1
Purposes of The NPEC ANSWERS Project

Describe and analyze information on frequently used surveys of postsecondary education institutions and national sample surveys
Promote better use of the national datasets
Provide a compendium of definitions and questions to promote best practices in survey development
Reduce data collection burden on institutions
Improve the comparability of data across surveys by promoting de facto standards

matrix tool from ANSWERS which allows users to select a broad subject area, then to pick more narrow terms that are within that subject to find related data. A sample screenshot is shown below, illustrating the search for enrollment data that break out freshmen profile information in the IPEDS Fall Enrollment (EF) survey.

Another special tool for locating data by topic is the SHEEO Online Access to Resources (SOAR) Web site, developed by the State Higher Education Executive Officers association. SOAR is "designed to support postsecondary education research and policy analysis" (http://www.sheeo.org/soar/).

SOAR allows users to search through two broad compendiums, "National Data Sources on Higher Education" and "Resources on Teacher Mobility." In addition to locating sources of data by seven broad topics and more than 50

Figure 2:
Search for Enrollment Data on Freshmen Profile

Matrix of Variables from National Surveys

Subjects:	Topics:	Datasets:	Variables:
Administration	(Enrollment)	(Freshmen Profile)	(IPEDS EF 01)
Admissions	Age	CDS 00	1st-time, 1st-yr students graduated HS past 12 mn
Assessment	Certificate	College Board 00	First-time first-year students (degree-seeking only)
Athletics	Classroom	IPEDS EF 00	State Residence of student when 1st admitted
Characteristics	Contact Hours	IPEDS EF 01	Status residence of first-time first-year students
Completions	Credit hours	IPEDS EF 94	
Crime	Demographics	IPEDS EF 95	
Discipline	Extension	IPEDS EF 96	
Enrollment	First Professional	IPEDS EF 97	
Equipment	Foreign Countries	IPEDS EF 98	
Ethnicity	Freshmen Profile	IPEDS IC 00	
Facilities	FTE	IPEDS IC 01	
Faculty	Graduate	IPEDS IC 94	
Finance	Headcount	IPEDS IC 95	
Financial Aid	Level	IPEDS IC 96	
Gender	Misc	IPEDS IC 97	
Hospital	Postdocs	IPEDS IC 98	
Instruction	Programs Offered	IPEDS IC 99	
Library	Remedial	IPEDS IPSFA 00	
Military	Residence		
Public Service	Status		
Research	Summer		
Respondents	Transfers		
Salaries	Undergraduate		
Staff			
Student Charges			
Student Services			
Survey			

keywords, SOAR describes each collection and provides links to key and related publications. The National Data Sources compendium is in its fifth edition and may be downloaded in PDF format. Its sections are broken into general references, students and learning, faculty and staff, finance and facilities, K-12, adult/workforce, and other resources. Additional search options in SOAR allow users to specify an organization/agency, state, or level (institutional, international, national, regional, or state). [1]

A second approach to locating data is by *source.* For example, a researcher may choose to investigate whether one of the federal agencies that collect postsecondary education-related data provides a dataset of interest. Most often, researchers use data and tools developed by NCES or the National Science Foundation (NSF). Many land grant institutions, and those with agricultural programs, also use data from the United States Department of Agriculture (USDA). There are many different types of online tools available from these agencies to facilitate the accessing and analyzing of their data.

The *level of aggregation* is a third lens used by researchers when locating data. At what level of aggregation does the researcher want to explore the data? Examples of levels of aggregation include state, region, Carnegie classification, individual institutions, and discipline. A sample survey about financial aid may not allow for analysis by state. Data from an institutional survey may be aggregated across schools to calculate a statewide figure, if the population of institutions is collected. Discipline-specific data may not always be available except in special studies or association surveys.

It is important for the researcher to separate the level of aggregation of the collection from the level of aggregation that the researcher is interested in for analysis. For example, in order to view tuition data by state, it is necessary to look at institutional data, because there is no collection of data from state offices.

Collection methods are a fourth lens to use in locating data. Are sample data adequate for the issue to be studied? Or are data needed for all individual institutions or departments or from a certain population? If sample data are to be used, is there sufficient stratification to make generalizations about the level of aggregation in which the user is interested? Even though a variable such as discipline is included in a survey, that does not necessarily mean that there is adequate weighting to perform every type of desired analysis. There are many other collection issues that must be addressed for a researcher to feel comfortable with the data. For example, how are missing data imputed and what is the response rate? These types of questions are further documented in section four.

Time, or *date*, is a fifth lens for locating data. Does the researcher want current data, three-year trends, historical data, or another view of the data with slices of time? It is important to document this need before looking for datasets. There are a number of very interesting longitudinal datasets available for looking at student cohorts, as well as science and engineering personnel, over time.

The sixth and final approach is determining *how the user wants to manipulate the data*. Sometimes, the user simply wants to download an extract for analysis locally using software tools such as SAS, SPSS, Access, or Excel. At other times, the data element dictionary and weighting scheme may be very complex. The user may then wish to use a software tool specific to the data. These more specific tools assist with merging multiple datasets over time, calculating new variables, developing appropriate weighting schemes for sample data, viewing frequencies by value label, and creating cross-tabs with descriptive statistics. While these can all be done with standard statistical software, some users prefer to use unique tools that will complete the entire task for them. Examples of unique tools include the Data Analysis Systems (DAS) from NCES and the WebCASPAR and SESTAT tools from NSF. These tools help users quickly understand a variety of collection issues.

In summary, when searching for data, it is important to review these six basic questions:

Table 2
Questions to Ask in Finding Data

What are the topics of interest?
Is a certain data source preferred?
What level of aggregation will be used for the results?
Are sample or population data needed?
Which data are available based upon the date/time period of interest?
Is the dataset all that is necessary, or are special tools for analysis needed?

Understanding Major Data Collections

Because of their importance in the determination of national trends and policy analysis, the major data collections, which are conducted by the primary federal agencies concerned with postsecondary education must be understood. Agencies conducting major data collections include the United States Department of Education, the NSF, and the USDA. Other federal and state agencies, national associations, organizations concerned with postsecondary education, institutions, and commercial vendors also collect data. This section is not exhaustive. Rather, the highlights of collections are presented to provide a broad overview of what is available. The focus is on datasets that are available to users for free, as well as in electronic format suitable for further analyses.

U.S. Department of Education

NCES conducts the majority of institutional surveys and sample surveys for the U.S. Department of Education. Other offices are involved in efforts such as the Campus Crime/Security Survey, Equity in Athletics, and financial aid administration. The range of data collections may be grouped by population surveys of institutions, sample surveys of institutions and departments, and sample surveys of individuals (i.e., faculty and students).

The Integrated Postsecondary Education Data System (IPEDS) surveys are at the heart of many NCES collection efforts. They are based on mandated reporting of more than 9,000 institutions and include hundreds of data elements. IPEDS replaced the Higher Education General Information Survey (HEGIS), which collected data from 1965 to 1986 on accredited institutions. HEGIS included components for Earned Degrees/Completions, Finance, Residence and Migration, Salaries, Fall Enrollment, and Institutional Characteristics.

Where IPEDS surveys were submitted via paper survey forms from 1986 through 1999, there are now three combined data collections that are administered online at different times during the year (Fall, Winter, and Spring). In each dataset, references are still made to the print equivalent surveys, many of which have existed since HEGIS.

Discipline-specific data are collected by Classification of Instructional Programs (CIP) code, a taxonomy unique to NCES. A CIP 2000 version of this taxonomy has replaced the 1990 document, after extensive field review. Use of the new CIP taxonomy will be mandatory by 2004. Additional information about CIP 2000 is available at: http://nces.ed.gov/ipeds/web2000/cip2000.asp.

A complete list of NCES descriptions of these individual IPEDS surveys is included in Table 3. General information about IPEDS is available at: http://nces.ed.gov/ipeds/index.html.

Table 3 also includes the many sample surveys that have been conducted by NCES over time. Most of these are completed by persons, although survey records are supplemented by other Department of Education records such as financial aid information. Postsecondary Education Quick Information System (PEQIS) studies have examined such topics as distance learning, remedial education, and disabled students.

National Science Foundation

NSF supports the collection of a number of postsecondary-related datasets, outlined in Table 4. Data are collected from surveys of institutions, departments and programs, federal agencies, and persons. The primary focus is on information about science and engineering, though some surveys such as the biennial Survey of Doctorate Recipients (SDR) have been expanded at times to include humanities disciplines. [2]

The SDR, National Survey of Recent College Graduates (NSRCG) and the National Survey of College Graduates (NSCG) make up a larger, integrated, biennial collection called the Scientist and Engineer Statistics (SESTAT) data system. Another sample survey, the Survey of Public Attitudes Toward and Understanding of Science and Technology, looks at the public's knowledge and perception of science and engineering including educational data. General

Table 3
Survey Datasets from NCES

TYPE	NAME	DESCRIPTION OF DATASET
Population - completed by school	IPEDS Institutional Characteristics (IC)	Institution names; addresses; telephone numbers; tuition, room and board charges; con-trol or affiliation; calendar system; levels of degrees and awards offered; types of pro-grams; selected student services; admission requirements; and accreditation status. IC surveys prior to 2000 collected instructional activity and unduplicated headcount data, which are now collected on the Enrollment survey.
Population - completed by school	IPEDS Fall Enrollment (EF)	Full- and part-time enrollment by racial/ethnic category and gender for undergraduate, first professional, and graduate student levels. Age distributions by student level and gender in odd numbered years. First time, first-year degree seeking student enrollments by home state of residence in even numbered years. Also in even-numbered years, four-year institutions are required to complete enrollment data by level, race/ethnicity, and gender for 9 selected disciplines for the Office for Civil Rights. In addition, the En-rollment survey now collects the instructional activity and unduplicated headcount data. Starting in 2002, unduplicated headcount by student level, and by race/ethnicity and gender of student are also be requested, as will total number of students in the entering class.
Population - completed by school	IPEDS Completions (C)	Numbers of associate's, bachelor's, master's, doctor's, and first professional degrees, and other formal awards, by field of study, and race/ethnicity and gender of recipient. Starting in 2001, completers of double majors by degree level, by race/ethnicity and gender of recipient, and by 6-digit CIP code will also be requested.
Population - completed by school	IPEDS Faculty Salaries (SA)	Full-time instructional faculty by rank, gender, tenure status, and length of contract; salaries and fringe benefits of fulltime instructional faculty. Data are collected annually, except for 2000.
Population - completed by school	IPEDS Fall Staff (S)	Number of institutional staff by occupational activity, full and part-time status, gender, and race/ethnicity. Data are collected in odd numbered years. Beginning with 1993, this survey replaced the EEO6 survey conducted by the Equal Employment Opportunity Commission.
Population - completed by school	IPEDS Employees by Assigned Position (EAP)	Headcount of full-time and part-time employees by faculty status and primary func-tion/occupational activity. New survey, optional for 2001-02.
Population - completed by school	IPEDS Finance (F)	Current fund revenues by source (e.g., tuition and fees, government, gifts); current fund expenditures by function (e.g., instruction, research); assets and indebtedness; and scholarship and fellowship awards. Since 1997, Finance data have collected in different formats based on the institution's accounting standards (FASB or GASB).
Population - completed by school	IPEDS Student Fi-nancial Aid (SFA)	Started as the Institutional Price and Student Financial Aid study in 1999. Includes the number and percent of full-time, first-time, degree/certificate-seeking undergraduate students receiving student financial aid, by type of aid.

Table 3
Survey Datasets from NCES

TYPE	NAME	DESCRIPTION OF DATASET
Population - completed by school	Academic Libraries (ALS)	Total library operating expenditures, full-time-equivalent library staff, service outlets, total volumes held at the end of the academic year, circulation, interlibrary loans, public service hours, patron count, reference transactions per typical week, and online services. Beginning in 1996, libraries were asked whether they offered the following electronic services: an electronic catalog that includes the library's holdings; electronic full-text periodicals; Internet access; library reference services by e-mail; and electronic docu-ment delivery to patron's account-address.
Population - completed by school	IPEDS Graduation Rates (GRS)	Number of students entering the institution as full-time, first-time, degree or certificate-seeking in a particular year (cohort), by race/ethnicity and gender; number completing within 150% of normal time to program completion; number transferred to other insti-tutions; number of students receiving athletically-related student aid in the cohort and number completing within 150% of normal time.
Population - completed by schools	Equity in Athletics Disclosure Act (EADA)	EADA requires the Secretary of Education to collect information and provide to Con-gress a report on financial and statistical information on men's and women's collegiate sports, including athletic participation, staffing, coaching salaries, and revenues and expenses. Comparable to the NCAA report.
Population - completed by schools	Campus Crime and Security at Post-secondary Education Institutions Survey	Annual campus security report by institution with data on alleged criminal offenses reported to campus security authorities or local police agencies. The data collected do not necessarily reflect prosecutions or convictions for crime. Broken out by type of crime and location.
Population - completed by schools	Fiscal Operations Report and Applica-tion to Participate (FISAP)	Data on campus-based financial aid programs, by institution.
Sample - completed by school	Postsecondary Edu-cation Quick Information System (PEQIS)	The PEQIS was established in 1991 to collect issue-oriented data quickly and with minimum response burden. PEQIS was designed to meet the data needs of Department of Education analysts, planners and decision makers when information could not be collected quickly through traditional NCES surveys. The data collected through PEQIS are representative at the national level. The PEQIS employs a standing sample of 1,500 postsecondary institutions.
Sample - com-pleted by person	Adult Education Survey (AES)	Part of the National Household Education Surveys Program (NHES) data collection system. Household membership and individual characteristics; participation in adult education; type of program (vocational, occupational, basic skills, etc.); reasons for taking courses and barriers to participation in adult education. AES collected in 91, 95, 99, and 01. The Adult Education and Lifelong Learning survey (AELL-NHES:2001) also asked about less formal learning at work.
Sample - com-pleted by person	Recent College Graduates (RCG)	Date of graduation; field of study; graduates newly qualified to teach; further enroll-ment; financial aid; employment status (especially teacher employment characteristics); job characteristics and earnings; age; marital status; sex; and race/ethnicity. The survey was conducted in 1976, 1978, 1981, 1985, 1987 and 1991. More recent data collections of a longitudinal nature are undertaken by B&B.

Table 3
Survey Datasets from NCES

TYPE	NAME	DESCRIPTION OF DATASET
Sample - completed by students, parents, & institutions	National Postsecondary Student Aid Study (NPSAS)	Includes data from three sources. From institutional student records: year in school; major field of study; type and control of institution; attendance status; tuition and fees; admission test scores; financial aid awards; cost of attendance; student budget information and expected family contribution for aided students; grade point average; age; date first enrolled. From student interviews, level; major field of study; financial aid at other schools attended during year; other sources of financial support; monthly expenses; reasons for selecting the school they are attending; current marital status; age; race/ethnicity; sex; highest degree expected; employment and income; community service. From parent survey: parents' marital status; age; highest level of education achieved; income; amount of financial support provided to children; types of financing used to pay child's educational expenses; occupation and industry.
Sample - see NPSAS	Baccalaureate and Beyond (B&B)	Follows an over-sample of graduating seniors from the National Postsecondary Student Aid Study. Includes information on education, employment, and other experiences. Collected current Federal aid and loan status information from ED records. B&B:93/94/97 included the collection of postsecondary transcripts. A new B&B cohort was created using NPSAS:2000 and this group was surveyed again in 2001 for the last time, similar to the RCG. B&B:93 will be studied again in 2003 with a focus on completion of graduate and professional school and educational indebtedness.
Sample - completed by students	Beginning Post-secondary Student Longitudinal Study (BPS)	BPS is designed specifically to collect data related to persistence in and completion of postsecondary education programs; relationships between work and education efforts; and the effect of postsecondary education on the lives of individuals. BPS has followed two cohorts. First time beginning students in a cohort from the NPSAS:90 were studied with follow-ups in 1992 and 1994. Beginners taken from NPSAS:96 ere were followed in 1998 and 2001. In addition to base-year NPSAS and all interview data, BPS: 96/98/2001 contains postsecondary entry test scores as well as financial aid records for the entire undergraduate period.
Sample - completed by faculty, chairs, & institutions	National Study of Postsecondary Faculty (NSOPF)	Includes data from three sources. From institutional survey: counts of faculty by rank; faculty hires and departures; tenure of faculty; tenure policies; retirement and other benefits for faculty. From department chair survey: faculty composition in department; tenure of faculty in department; tenure policies; rank; gender, and minority/non-minority status of faculty in department; faculty hires and departures in department; hiring practices; activities to assess faculty performance; professional and developmental activities. From faculty survey: socio-demographic characteristics; academic and professional background; field of instruction; employment history; current employment status including rank and tenure; outside employment; workload; courses taught; job satisfaction and attitudes; career and retirement plans; benefits and compensation.
Sample - completed by students	National Longitudinal Study of the H.S. Class of 1972 (NLS-72)	NLS-72 describes the transition of young adults from high school through postsecondary education and the workplace. This is considered the "grandmother" of the longitudinal studies conducted by NCES. Participants in the study were selected when they were seniors in high school in the spring of 1972, and in a supplementary sample drawn in 1973. The records include the "Base Year" survey; follow-up surveys in 1973, 1974, 1976, 1979, and 1986; high school records; and postsecondary transcripts (collected in 1984).

131

Table 3
Survey Datasets from NCES

Sample - completed by students	National Education Longitudinal Study of 1988 (NELS:88)	Beginning with an 8th grade cohort in 1988, NELS:88 provides trend data about critical transitions experienced by young people as they develop, attend school, and embark on their careers. Data were collected from students and their parents, teachers, and high school principals and from existing school records such as high school transcripts. Cognitive tests (math, science, reading, and history) were administered during the base year (1988), first follow-up (1990), and second follow-up (1992). A third follow-up was conducted in 1994. All dropouts were retained in the study. The final follow-up of NELS:88 was conducted in 2000 and also includes the collection of postsecondary transcripts. This allows examination of the educational and labor market outcomes of the initial eighth-grade cohort of 1988 in the year 2000, when the majority of the cohort was 26 years old.
Sample - completed by students	High School and Beyond (HS&B)	HS&B describes the activities of seniors and sophomores as they progressed through high school, postsecondary education, and into the workplace. The data cover the period 1980 through 1992 and include parent, teacher, and high school transcript data, student financial aid records, and college transcripts in addition to student questionnaires. The HS&B survey included two cohorts: the 1980 senior class, and the 1980 sophomore class. Both cohorts were surveyed every two years through 1986, and the 1980 sopho-more class was also surveyed again in 1992.

information about NSF data collections is available at: http://www.nsf.gov/sbe/srs/survey.htm.

Sample surveys are designed to provide national estimates for certain groups or activities. There are a number of publications driven by their production. NSF surveys have a unique taxonomy of disciplines, often in a finer level of detail than CIP codes for science and engineering fields. These come from the Survey of Earned Doctorates (SED) data on field of degree. The field or discipline of work documented in the SESTAT surveys are at a much less fine level of detail and match the occupation codes use by the U.S. Census Bureau. When working with disciplinary data, users will have to understand the crosswalk between the dataset they are using and their own departments or programs, which may be unique combinations of CIP or NSF taxonomies.

NSF's datasets place heavy emphasis on understanding the characteristics of doctoral scientists and engineers in the United States. These survey samples are taken from the Doctorate Records File (DRF), a database currently maintained by the National Opinion Research Center of the University of Chicago under contract to NSF. The DRF dates back to 1920, with the collection of graduation announcements and lists. The SED was begun in 1958 to continue

Table 4
Survey Datasets from NSF

TYPE	NAME	DESCRIPTION OF DATASET
Population - completed by schools	Graduate Students and Postdoctorates in Science and Engineering (GSS)	Counts of graduate students by academic institution, department or program, geographic location, highest degree granted by institution (doctorate/master's), institutional control (public versus private), enrollment status, level of study (first year, beyond first year), sex, race/ethnicity, citizenship, primary source of financial support (e.g., NSF, NIH, etc.) of full-time students, primary mechanism of financial support (e.g., fellowship, research assistantship, etc.) of full-time students. Counts of postdoctoral fellows and doctoral non-faculty research staff by academic institution, geographic location, highest degree granted by institution, institutional control, sex, and for postdoctorates, source of support and citizenship.
Population - completed by grads	Survey of Earned Doctorates Awarded in the United States (SED)	Sex; age; race/ethnicity; marital status; citizenship; disabilities; dependents; specialty field of doctorate; all institutions attended from high school to completion of doctorate; time spent in completion of doctorate; source of financial support for graduate study; education debt incurred; postdoctoral plans; educational attainment of parents.
Population - completed by federal agencies	Survey of Federal Funds for Research and Development (FFR&D)	Character of work (basic research, applied research, and development), Federal agency, Federal funds for research and development, Federal obligations (defined by initiating agency), Federal outlays for research and development, Federally-funded research and development centers (FFRDC), Field of science and engineering, Geographic location (within U.S.), Performer (type of organization doing work, i.e., intramural, extramural), R&D plant.
Population - completed by federal agencies	Survey of Federal Science and Engineering Support to Universities, Colleges, & Nonprofit Institutions	Academic institution, Federal agency, Geographic location (within U.S.), Highest degree granted, Historically Black Colleges and Universities, Obligations (defined by obligating agency), R&D plant, Type of academic institution (Historically Black Institutions/others), Type of activity (e.g., research and development; S&E instructional facilities), Type of institutional control
Population - completed by schools	Survey of Research and Development Expenditures at Universities and Col-leges (Academic R&D)	Academic institution, Character of work (basic research, applied research, and development), Equipment Expenditures, Expenditures for S&E R&D, FFRDCs, Field of science and engineering (for Total and Federal sources only), Geographic location (within U.S.), Highest degree granted, Passed through funds (through the institution to subrecipients and also institution received as a subrecipient), Source of funds (Federal, State and local, industry, institutional, and other), Type of academic institution (doctorate-granting versus non-doctorate-granting), Type of academic institution (Historically Black Institutions versus others), Type of institutional control.

Table 4
Survey Datasets from NSF

TYPE	NAME	DESCRIPTION OF DATASET
Sample - completed by persons w/ S&E doctorates	Survey of Doctorate Recipients (SDR)	Citizenship, Country of birth, Country of citizenship, Year of birth, Disability status, Educational history, Employed status (part-time, full-time), Employer size, Faculty rank, Field of degree(s), Geographic place of employment, Labor force status (employed, unemployed, not in labor force), Level of degree(s), Marital status, Number and age of children, Occupation, Second job, Postdoc indicator, Primary work activity (e.g., teaching, basic research, etc.), Race/ethnicity, Salary, Hours/weeks worked, Previous year earned income, Professional association membership, School enrollment status, Sector of employment (academia, industry, government), Sex, Tenure status.
Sample - completed by persons with S&E bachelor & master's degrees	National Survey of Recent College Graduates (NSRCG)	Citizenship, Country of birth, Country of citizenship, Year of birth, Disability status, Educational history, Employed status (part-time, full-time), Employer size, Field of degree(s), Geographic place of employment, Labor force status (employed, unemployed, not in labor force), Level of degree(s), Marital status, Number and age of children, Occupation, Second job, Primary work activity (e.g., teaching, basic research, etc.), Race/ethnicity, Salary, Hours/weeks worked, Previous year earned income, Professional association membership, School enrollment status, Sector of employment (academia, industry, government), Sex, GPA, Undergraduate debt.
Sample - completed by persons w/ at least a bachelors degree	National Survey of College Graduates (NSCG)	Citizenship, Country of birth, Country of citizenship, Age, Disability status, Educational history, Employed status (part-time, full-time), Employer size, Field of degree(s), Geographic place of employment, Labor force status (employed, unemployed, not in labor force), Level of degree(s), Marital status, Number and age of children, Occupation, Second job, Primary work activity (e.g., teaching, basic research, etc.), Race/ethnicity, Salary, Hours/weeks worked, Previous year earned income, Professional association membership, School enrollment status, Sector of employment (academia, industry, government), Sex.
Sample - completed by schools	Survey of Science and Engineering Research Facilities	Amount of S&E research space; adequacy of the amount of S&E research space; condition of S&E research space; completion costs and NASF of repair/renovation and construction of S&E research space; source of funding for repair/renovation and construction of S&E re-search space; planned repair/renovation and construction of S&E research space; deferred repair/renovation and construction of S&E research space. Other non-survey variables: whether institution awards doctorate degrees in S&E, HBCU status, whether public or private institution.
Sample - completed by persons	Survey of Public Attitudes	Acceptance of science and technology, Admiration of science and technology, Age, Attitudes towards science and technology policy areas, Educational level, Geographic location (within U.S.), Interest in science and technology, Occupation, Perceived impacts of science and technology, Personal activities regarding science and technology, Public knowledge about science and technology, Race/ethnicity, Sex.

134

this data collection. The SED is administered through graduate school deans and completed by all graduates with Ph.D., Sc.D., Ed.D., Doctor of Arts, and other types of doctoral degrees. Professional school doctorates such as medicine, dentistry, and veterinary medicine are not included. There are approximately 1.4 million records in the 1920-2000 DRF.

Data on science and engineering programs by discipline at individual institutions are collected in the Survey of Graduate Students and Postdoctorates in Science and Engineering (GSS), the Survey of Research and Development Expenditures at Universities and Colleges (Academic R&D), and the Survey of Scientific and Engineering Research Facilities (R&D Facilities). Federal agencies submit data regarding specific postsecondary education institutions to NSF through two collections: the Survey of Federal Science and Engineering Support

Table 5
Survey Datasets from USDA

TYPE	NAME	DESCRIPTION OF DATASET
Population - completed by schools	Agriculture, Renew-able Natural Re-sources and Forestry - Enrollment	Available for Two-Year, Baccalaureate, Masters and Doctoral enrollment in Baccalaureate granting Colleges of Agriculture, Renewable Natural Resources and Forestry. Historic information is available from 1984. Data are summarized by the following categories: institution, academic area, gender, minority, land grant affiliation (1862, 1890, Non-Land Grant), professional, and NASULGC defined region.
Population - completed by schools	Agriculture, Renew-able Natural Re-sources and Forestry - Degrees Awarded	Degrees conferred information is available for Two-Year, Baccalaureate, Masters and Doctoral enrollment in Baccalaureate granting Colleges of Agriculture, Renewable Natural Resources and Forestry. Historic information is available from 1984. Data are summarized by the following categories: institution, academic area, gender, minority, affiliation (1862, 1890, Non-Land Grant), professional , and NASULGC defined region.
Population - completed by schools	Agriculture, Renewable Natural Re-sources and Forestry - Placement	Information summarizes the placement of Baccalaureate, Masters and Doctoral graduates in the agricultural, renewable natural resource and forestry sciences. Information is provided using academic area of degree granted and placement cluster. Placement clus-ters identified were based on Bureau of Labor Statistics area of work categories. Aver-age starting salaries for graduates placed is also summarized by academic area of degree granted.
Population - completed by schools	Agriculture, Renewable Natural Resources and Forestry - Faculty	Provided for resident instruction faculty only. New faculty hired information is available annually. Annual salary information by broad academic area is available annually. Comprehensive information (collected every five years) summarizes a variety of demographic characteristics for resident instruction faculty in Colleges of Agriculture, Renewable Natural Resources and Forestry.

Table 5
Survey Datasets from USDA

TYPE	NAME	DESCRIPTION OF DATASET
Population - completed by schools	Agriculture, Renewable Natural Resources and Forestry - Institutional Information	Attributes for all degree granting (Baccalaureate and higher) institutions in the agricultural, renewable natural resource and forestry sciences. Names, addresses, phone, fax, and email information are available for administrative contacts in Colleges of Agriculture, Renewable Natural Resources and Forestry (Dean, Associate Dean and Assistant Dean levels). Information for these files is assimilated from information reported to FAEIS on an annual basis through professional association directories.
Population - completed by schools	Family and Consumer Sciences - Enrollment	Enrollment information is available for Two-Year, Baccalaureate, Masters and Doctoral enrollment in Baccalaureate granting Colleges/Schools/Units of Family and Consumer Sciences. This survey is initiated biennially. Data are summarized by the following categories: academic area, gender, minority status and professional association.
Population - completed by schools	Family and Consumer Sciences - Degrees Awarded	Degrees conferred information is available for Two-Year, Baccalaureate, Masters and Doctoral enrollment in Baccalaureate granting Colleges/Schools/Units of Family and Consumer Sciences. This survey is initiated biennially. Data are summarized by the following categories: academic area, gender, minority and professional association.
Population - completed by schools	Family and Consumer Sciences - Faculty	Provided for resident instruction faculty only. New faculty hired information is available annually. Current faculty information (collected annually) summarizes a variety of demographic characteristics for resident instruction faculty in Colleges/Schools/Units of Family and Consumer Sciences.
Population - completed by schools	Family and Consumer Sciences - Institutional Information	Names, addresses, phone, fax, email information are available for contacts in Colleges/Schools/Units of Family and Consumer Sciences. Information for these files is assimilated from information reported to FAEIS on an annual basis through professional association directories.

to Universities, Colleges, & Nonprofit Institutions (Federal Support); and the Survey of Federal Funds for Research and Development (Federal Funds).

U.S. Department of Agriculture

The office of Higher Education Programs (HEP) is part of the Cooperative State Research, Education, and Extension Service of the United States Department of Agriculture. As one of its many activities, HEP maintains the Food and Agricultural Education Information System (FAEIS). FAEIS provides statistical information about postsecondary education related to the food and agricultural sciences. These disciplines include agriculture, forestry, renewable natural resources, family and consumer sciences, veterinary medicine, and closely allied fields.

Some of the data for FAEIS is secondary, compiled from the collections of professional associations, such as the American Association of Veterinary Medical Colleges. HEP also collects survey data of its own under two disciplinary clusters: (1) Agriculture, Renewable Natural Resources, and Forestry; and (2) Family and Consumer Sciences. Data are collected about enrollment, degrees awarded, faculty, placement, and institutional information. General information about these collections is available at: http://faeis.usda.gov.

Table 5 documents these HEP datasets.

Other Major Data Collections

There are many hundreds of postsecondary-related surveys and data collections. A much smaller number of these are accepted as de facto standards that may be relied upon for quality data. Some of these quality datasets originate from national associations, such as the American Association of University Professors (AAUP). They are targeted to specific audiences within the postsecondary education community or address specific policy issues, such as faculty salaries, and studies of tenure and rank.

The collection of postsecondary education data is a very viable commercial enterprise. A number of vendors, from John Minter Associates to *U.S. News and World Report*, collect, repackage, and sell data in various formats for different readers and data users. The quality and accuracy of these commercial collections has increased considerably as a result of the Common Data Set Initiative (CDS), a collaborative effort among data providers and publishers.

According to the CDS Web site, "The CDS is a set of standards and definitions of data items rather than a survey instrument or set of data represented in a database. Each of the postsecondary education surveys conducted by the participating publishers incorporates items from the CDS as well as unique items proprietary to each publisher."

The primary CDS vendors have included the College Board, Peterson's, *U.S. News & World Report*, and Wintergreen/Orchard House. Other CDS Advisory Board members include representatives from the following associations: the American Association of Community Colleges (AACC); the Association of American Collegiate Registrars and Admission Officers (AACRAO); the Association for Institutional Research (AIR); the National Association for College Admission Counseling (NACAC); the National Association of College and University Business Officers (NACUBO); the National Association of Independent Colleges and Universities (NAICU); and the National Association of Student Financial Aid Administration (NASFAA). Wintergreen/Orchard House has since withdrawn from this effort. Additional information is available at: http://www.commondataset.org/.

In using a dataset, the reliability and integrity of the collection must be assessed. If the survey developer incorporates CDS standards and definitions, along with those maintained by NCES and NSF, there is an obvious degree of quality. Users should be cautious about using datasets which purport to collect new types of interesting information but fail to maintain effective practices of survey design, such as the use of standard census dates and definitions and building on the integrity of existing federal collections.

Table 6 lists a sampling of these reliable datasets. The listing is not exhaustive and is not a statement about the quality of other datasets that are

Table 6
A Sample of Other National Datasets

AGENCY	SURVEY	DESCRIPTION OF DATASET
American Association of University Professors (AAUP)	Annual Faculty Compensation Survey [AAUP-FCS}	Faculty salaries, benefits, and tenure status by institution, rank, and gender
Association of Post-secondary Education Facilities Officers (APPA)	Comparative Costs and Staffing Report for Educa-tional Facilities	Facilities operations, energy & utilities, contracting/outsourcing, maintenance staffing, custodial and grounds operations, etc.
Association of Research Libraries (ARL)	ARL Statistics Questionnaire	Collections, expenditures, personnel, and public services
Chronicle of Higher Education	Facts & Figures. Almanac.	Miscellaneous institutional data from various sources, some collected by he Chronicle. Data include, but are not limited to, information about campus crime, faculty salaries, pay and benefits of college presidents, endowments, fundraising, research library holdings, government grants, gender equity in athletics, graduation rates, stipends and benefits for graduate students, student enrollment and characteristics, and tuition and fees.
College and University Personnel Association (CUPA)	Administrative Compensation Survey	Salaries and compensation data for administrators.
College and University Personnel Association (CUPA)	Mid-Level Administra-tive/Professional Salary Survey	Salaries and compensation data for mid-level administrative and professional personnel
College and University Personnel Association (CUPA)	National Faculty Salary Survey By Discipline and Rank	Separate public and private institution versions of this survey of faculty salaries by discipline and rank. Information on new assistant professor salaries.
College Board, The (CB)	Annual Survey of Colleges	Admissions; enrollment; transfer; expenses; financial aid; curriculum; international; faculty; graduate programs.
Council for Aid to Education (CAE)	Voluntary Support of Education	Gift income broken down by source, purpose and outright vs. deferred, with additional detail on numbers of donors and forms of giving.
Council of Graduate Schools (CGS)	CGS/GRE Survey of Graduate Enrollment	Enrollment, applications, and degrees
National Research Council (NRC)	Research-Doctorate Programs in the United States	Information on 3,634 programs in 41 fields at 274 universities that participated in a comprehensive study of the research-doctorate enterprise. Behind these data is a much larger information set containing details on 88,000 faculty members; 1 million publication, citation, and research grant records; and 16,000 questionnaires for the reputational survey of faculty quality and program effectiveness.

Table 6
A Sample of Other National Datasets

AGENCY	SURVEY	DESCRIPTION OF DATASET
Peterson's	Annual Survey of Graduate and Professional Institutions and Units	General institutional information, enrollment, faculty, research affiliations and projects, library and computer facilities, expenses, housing, financial aid/support, student services, degree programs, application and acceptance, entrance and degree requirements, degrees awarded, and contacts.
Peterson's	Annual Survey of Undergraduate Institutions	General institutional information, enrollment, persistence, freshman admissions, academics (e.g., faculty counts by status and gender; special programs; graduation requirements; etc.), facilities and services, expenses (e.g., full- and part-time tuition and fees and room and board; tuition payment plans and waivers), campus life, undergraduate majors; contacts, etc.
U.S. News	Rankings and Guides	Undergraduate, graduate, and professional school rankings and guides with extensive data collection.
University of Oklahoma	Consortium for Student Retention Data Exchange Survey	Enrollment and retention data.

not listed.   Rather, it was prepared initially as part of the NPEC ANSWERS project. The datasets are available for free or for sale at low cost in electronic format and are recognized as adhering to de facto standards and definitions.

Getting Access to Datasets

Once a dataset of interest has been located, there are several steps to consider in evaluating whether or not it will meet a user's needs. It is particularly useful to look at a copy of the actual survey instrument. The ANSWERS Web site includes links to each survey instrument and dataset; this is a good place to start. NCES, NSF, and USDA all provide links to their surveys. When using a dataset for the first time, it is helpful to match the data to those submitted by a specific institution using the same instrument. While the data dictionary is usually very clear, with a detailed description of each field and its possible value labels, there is no substitute for the importance of recognizing data that are in the right place on a form and in a dataset.

General information about each dataset should be reviewed, such as the number and type of respondents, year of administration, and how the data are made available. If the user does not want to analyze data using SAS, SPSS, or another statistical analysis software package, or needs a specialized query tool that is tailored to the dataset, it is much better to determine this at the outset.

IPEDS datasets are available in fixed, ASCII text format, with instructions for importing the data into Microsoft Access or Excel and for importing the data into SAS or SPSS with a "read" program. Those with multiple records per institution require more manipulation.   As part of the DAS software and separately, with its own installed software, Electronic Code Books (ECB) are available for each of the sample surveys, as well as for IPEDS. The most current IPEDS ECB is 2000, which is based on the most recent adjudicated,

Table 7
Online Access to Federal Datasets

AGENCY	COLLECTION/TOOL	WEB SITE
IAED for NCES	HEGIS datasets	http://www.icpsr.umich.edu/IAED/SERIES/hegis.html
IAED for NCES	Older IPEDS datasets	http://www.icpsr.umich.edu/IAED/SERIES/ipeds.html
NCES	Older IPEDS datasets	http://nces.ed.gov/ipeds/data.html
NCES	IPEDS Peer Analysis System	http://nces.ed.gov/ipedspas/
NCES	IPEDS COOL	http://nces.ed.gov/ipeds/cool/
NCES	IPEDS Electronic Code Books	http://nces.ed.gov/ipeds/ElectronicCodebook/i2000/
NCES	Academic Library Peer Comparison Tool	http://nces.ed.gov/surveys/libraries/academicpeer/
NCES	PEQIS	http://nces.ed.gov/pubsearch/getpubcats.asp?sid=016
NCES	NEDRC Table Library	http://nces.ed.gov/surveys/npsas/table_library/
NCES	NCES Quick Tables and Figures	http://nces.ed.gov/quicktables/
NCES	Data Analysis Systems (DAS)	http://nces.ed.gov/das/htm/surveys.html
NCES	DAS Electronic Code Books	http://nces.ed.gov/das/htm/das/ecb.html
IAED for NCES	IAED SDA/DAS for RCG survey	http://www.icpsr.umich.edu/IAED/das.html#iaed
IAED for NCES	HS&B survey data through 1986	http://www.icpsr.umich.edu/IAED/SERIES/hsb.html
IAED for NCES	RCG survey data before 1991	http://www.icpsr.umich.edu/IAED/SERIES/rcg.html
IAED for NCES	NLS.72 survey data	http://www.icpsr.umich.edu/IAED/SERIES/nls.html
OPE	OPE Campus Security Statistics	http://ope.ed.gov/SECURITY/OPEHome.asp
NSF	WebCASPAR	http://caspar.nsf.gov/
NSF	Public Use Data Files - GSS	http://www.nsf.gov/sbe/srs/gss99pub/start.htm
NSF	Academic Institutional Profiles	http://www.nsf.gov/sbe/srs/profiles/start.htm
NSF	SESTAT	http://srsstats.sbe.nsf.gov/
NSF	Science and Engineering Indicators	http://www.nsf.gov/sbe/srs/seind/start.htm
USDA	FAEIS	http://faeis.usda.gov

official, and final release IPEDS data. These ECBs let users browse, select, and view data elements, including the variable name, label, description, and value labels. Frequencies are also provided, along with minimum, maximum, mean, and standard deviation for continuous data elements. Whenever possible, users should obtain the codebook, or data element dictionary, for a dataset, including value labels and frequencies. Users may want to download ECBs from the NCES site to learn more about a dataset. However, if the DAS is being used for sample surveys, this is a duplication of the functionality, since the ECB is already built into the DAS.

Most of the federally funded datasets which have been "officially" released have been adjudicated, passing stringent error checks and guidelines as part of the preparation of mandated reports or tables. The institutional-level IPEDS datasets are mandated and may have imputed values for missing records or variables. None of the sample surveys include imputed data. The use of sample studies, in conjunction with IPEDS, allows for national estimates. Non-adjudicated data are not appropriate for national estimates, but are still useful for peer analysis and other type of internal studies. Likewise, the early release data which are available from the IPEDS Peer Analysis System are also appropriate for this level of study – with a notation that the data are not adjudicated or official. A researcher must know when the use of data is appropriate.

Table 7 lists Web sites where users may obtain free access to federal datasets about postsecondary education that are collected by the U.S. Department of Education, the National Science Foundation, and the U.S. Department of Agriculture.

U.S. Department of Education

While many IPEDS datasets are available for download from the NCES Web site with different tools, the International Archive of Education Data (IAED) is funded by NCES to be the source for older IPEDS, HEGIS, and sample survey data. The Archive is housed in and operated by the Inter-University Consortium for Political and Social Research (ICPSR) at the University of Michigan. Its purpose is to "preserve all of the NCES public-use research data holdings and make these holdings, as resources permit, suitably available for research throughout the nation and the world." Machine-readable codebooks, documentation, and datasets are provided for free with online registration. The Archive is available at: http://www.icpsr.umich.edu/IAED/.

Some IPEDS datasets are available in zipped format, dating back to the early days of Gopher and the World Wide Web. Previously, the data were available on magnetic tape and on floppy disk from the National Education Data Resource Center (NEDRC), under contract to NCES. Since 2000, NCES has published all newly released data, as well as a growing amount of historical data, in its IPEDS Peer Analysis System. Currently, data from 1985 and 1990 to present are available. With the Peer Analysis System, users may select data, create calculated variables, and create unique datasets for different institutions. Another option is to download each table (or section of survey data) directly in comma-separated, CSV text format. The IPEDS Peer Analysis System is currently being redesigned and will include a new "dataset-cutting tool" for creating unique datasets. A set of tutorials about using the Peer Tool are available at: http://nces.ed.gov/ipeds/tutorials/.

A more user-friendly version of these data at the individual institution level, designed to meet the mandates of Congress and its College Cost Report for three years of price and cost data, is the IPEDS College Opportunities On-Line tool (COOL). IPEDS COOL also provides a link to access to Campus Security/ Crime data for each institution. The Department of Education's Office of Postsecondary Education maintains a Web site with a searchable database of

Campus Security/Crime data. Similarly, NCES makes data on academic libraries available with another searchable online database.

NCES sample data are available in public use files as part of Data Analysis Systems (DAS) and in restricted access files, which require a site license and special conditions of use designed to protect confidentiality. The DAS works two ways: (1) locally on the user's computer using software and data installed via download or CD-Rom; and (2) by uploading/FTPing a DAS query from the same software to a special DAS server, where it is run and then made available for download on the DAS FTP site. While everything else is identical, the downloadable version does not allow users to create locally on the user's computer. New versions of the DAS are released periodically as different software packages. While also provided on CD-Rom, the software available for downloading is kept more current with important updates, corrections, and recodes. The DAS for PEQIS requires a restricted use site license. In addition, IAED provides DAS-like software with its Survey Documentation & Analysis (SDA) System, but only for the Recent College Graduates, 1991 sample survey.

Information about the sample surveys has also been compiled into a library of tables and is available as part of the NEDRC Table Library and the NCES Quick Tables and Figures tool. The results of NCES PEQIS surveys are also arrayed in this format. This Web site application is available at: http://nces.ed.gov/quicktables/.

National Science Foundation

NSF's three SESTAT sample surveys (SDR, NSCG, and NSCRG) are provided to the public through a special online tool, with extensive documentation of value labels, frequencies, and changes in the data element dictionaries over time. A restricted use site license is also available for any of these sample survey datasets, plus the SED and the Survey of Public Attitudes.

Two of the three NSF institutional surveys (GSS and Academic R&D), the data collected from federal agencies, and the SED are made available through the online WebCASPAR tool. Developed originally in the early 1990's as a CD-ROM subscription service and software for analyzing datasets, WebCASPAR has evolved to a dynamic and powerful dataset tool. Just as with the IPEDS Peer Tool, users may select standard reports, create customized reports, select institutions based on criteria, and save customized reports that they create. Users who wish to create a dataset should locate the variables of interest and save the data for all available institutions.

Where IPEDS uses a list of checkboxes across multiple pages of selections to choose options and variables, WebCASPAR also allows users to visually diagram a cross-tab report, cutting and pasting different fields into the report structure to meet their needs. The GSS is available as public use datasets as well and there is a "Guide to the Data Files" that documents the data availability, distribution, and code structure.

WebCASPAR includes some important non-NSF sponsored data as well, including most of the long-standing, historical IPEDS datasets and two years of information from the National Research Council's data collection about Research-Doctorate Programs. A tutorial and discussion group is also provided.

Another useful NSF Web site is the online documentation of "Academic Institutional Profiles." These profiles incorporate all data available through different institutional surveys, and array the results over time for a single institution. This is a valuable way of quickly viewing the types and years of NSF data available for a university, in order to know whether to further explore a dataset. Another way is to view the "Data Map" feature in WebCASPAR, which documents data sources by subject, organization, variable, category, and academic institution.

Information about the Survey of Public Attitudes is available as table results in the Science and Engineering Indicators publication series and Web site. A restricted use site license is available, and a public use version should soon be available on CD-Rom.

U.S. Department of Agriculture

The Food and Agricultural Education Information System (FAEIS) provides online data in two broad disciplinary clusters: agriculture, renewable natural resources and forestry; and family and consumer sciences. The data are analyzed and available in different levels of aggregation, including: national, institution, degree level, academic area of specialization, race/ethnicity, gender, region, type of institution, 1862 and 1890 Land Grant status, non-Land Grants, and by institutional membership in professional associations. The data are provided online in different formats, including graphical images and Adobe PDF files. Users may request electronic versions of the data, at no charge, suitable for additional analyses, by emailing FAEIS staff. For more information, see http://faeis.usda.gov.

Other National Datasets

Some survey developers make their datasets available to institutional researchers and policy analysts, although it is sometimes necessary to hand-enter information from print publications or PDF files. Of the four publishers originally involved in the Common Dataset Initiative, the College Board is the only one which will sell the data directly to institutions and states for internal use. The cost is contingent on the usage. In the past, Wintergreen/Orchard House data were sold at a much greater cost to commercial clients such as insurance companies and other publishers.

Peterson's and *U.S. News & World Report* make much of the data used in their print publications available on the Web. Users who wish to use these data should seriously consider cutting and pasting data variables by institution from these sites. Wintergreen/Orchard House supplies data on a much larger, commercial scale to interested parties, such as insurance companies and directories.

The *Chronicle of Higher Education* is an invaluable source for institutional datasets with its "Facts and Figures" and Almanac sections. For example, the *Chronicle* contains a searchable database of historical data about Crime on College Campuses, broken down by state and institution. Users may save these online pages, and readily view them in Excel, for further manipulation and analysis. Some of the other *Chronicle* data of interest include information about faculty salaries, compensation of college presidents, endowments, fundraising, research library holdings, government grants, gender equity in athletics, graduation rates, stipends and benefits for graduate students, and tuition and fees.

Institutions which participate in special data collections such as AAUP, APPA, CUPA, and disciplinary surveys usually benefit from receiving a copy of the data in print or electronic format. The AAUP Faculty Compensation Survey Report and the March/April issue of *Academe* are examples. Even if the entire dataset is not for sale, schools may obtain copies of a survey submission from peer institutions and use the results for internal analysis. Some private associations among institutions, such as the *Postsecondary Education Data Sharing Consortium*, collect data from multiple sources and repackage them for its members. For more information, see http://hedsftp.fandm.edu/.

Other Considerations in Manipulating Datasets

With WebCASPAR and the IPEDS Peer Tool, there is no need for the user to worry about merging multiple datasets or a single dataset across multiple years, because the software builds in this capability. SESTAT requires users to select the year of data; the system then handles merges between the SDR, NSCG, and NSCRG seamlessly, because these are essentially the same survey with three different populations and only slight variations in content.

The manipulation of individual IPEDS, HEGIS, and other datasets is not always straightforward. Usually, the data are stored in tables, so that columns of data are related to specific questions or cells on the source survey. The variables, or fields, are named with a standard naming convention that makes intuitive sense to users, given the location of the variable on the survey instrument and/or the type of data. It is important for a researcher to know how a survey instrument has changed during time, including the availability of key variables of interest, as well as how these variables are coded, recoded, and reported in the dataset.

Where the complexity of the survey or its length dictates, multiple data files or tables may be used. Each file provides a specific section of the survey (*i.e.,* Part B – Expenditures of the IPEDS Finance Survey data file). For all IPEDS files, the Institutional Characteristics survey provides all identifying information for an institution, such as Carnegie classification, location, and control. All other IPEDS files are linked to the Institutional Characteristics, or IC, file by the institution's unique identifier or UNITID. For many NSF datasets in WebCASPAR, and for older HEGIS files, the unique identifier is Federal

Interagency Committee on Education (FICE) code. For the NSF GSS, there are multiple submissions from an institution for each graduate program by degree level. The IPEDS Fall Staff Survey is more difficult than other IPEDS files to use as a dataset, a result of the use of multiple records for each "line."

The issue of identifying institutions is especially important when using data from multiple sources, such as IPEDS, AAUP, and a disciplinary association. Each survey developer may collect data from a different administrative unit on a campus. While UNITID or FICE may be the lowest level of identification for an institution, some departments or programs may exist in a consortia of institutions. Datasets which rely on FICE codes alone, or, worse, institutional name, may limit the user in their utility for merging to other sources. Hospitals may have their own identifiers. Systems, branch campuses, and off-site locations may be treated differently, depending upon the policy and training of the office which completed the survey at the time.

Table 8
ANSWERS Survey Developer Information

EVERYTHING YOU NEED TO KNOW ABOUT A DATASET
Data Collection
What is the purpose of this survey?
What topical domains are covered (i.e. admissions, enrollment, faculty)?
Does the survey reference data gathered by another organization? If so, what data elements are duplication.
What specific times of the year does the survey reference?
How long has the survey been administered?
How frequently is the survey administered?
Is there an electronic data collection instrument?
Respondent Information
What types of schools are surveyed (i.e. Carnegie, control, degree programs)?
What types of schools respond to the survey?
Does the survey instrument vary by type of school? If so, how ?
What is the average, overall response rate (over 3 years)?
What is the most recent response rate?
Which office usually receives the survey?
Which office usually coordinates the collection of survey data?
When is the survey sent to respondents?

145

Table 8
ANSWERS Survey Developer Information

EVERYTHING YOU NEED TO KNOW ABOUT A DATASET
When is the survey due? If the date is usually extended, to what date?
How long does it take a typical respondent to complete the survey (in hours)?
Are there any scheduled follow-ups to non-respondents?
Are there any enticements offered for responding (i.e. cash, free report)?
Reporting/Data Availability
Do you involve schools in editing or reviewing the data?
Do the data require a significant amount of editing/cleaning?
How are missing/non-response data handled? Imputation method?
How long after the due date are the data available in some format?
Are the electronic data publicly or commercially available? If so, where, when, in what format, and at what cost?
Are reports about the data available online? If so, where, when, in what format, and at what cost?
Are reports about the data available in print? If so, where, when, and at what cost?
What are current titles of publications based on the survey data?
What is the future of the survey?
How successful is the survey in meeting the data needs of its target audience?

NCES and NSF both expend a great deal of effort tracking institutional changes over time, resulting from mergers, closures, changes in institutional mission, and name changes. This is the benefit of allowing NCES and NSF to keep track of multiple datasets through the IPEDS Peer Tool and WebCASPAR.

Everything a Researcher Needs to Know about a Dataset
There are a number of things about a dataset, which the researcher learns only after years of use. For example, data for a peer institution may change

146

unexpectedly across several years, for no known reason. The user may never know that the peer institution changed student information systems or that a report was prepared by different people over time using different programming techniques, who did not anticipate how the data would be used. Another frequent problem in systems is a change in the use of value labels for a variable. An institutional researcher may request an extract to submit for a collection, never knowing that the screen design for the system may change the use of a value label, changing the meaning to something entirely different than expected.

As part of the NPEC ANSWERS tools, these relatively unknown aspects of each national dataset are better documented. Eventually, as users work with a particular dataset, they will want to make sure they understand these issues and concerns.

Emerging Trends in Data Collection

The past few years have seen a dramatic change in data collection, moving instruments from paper to the Web. This chapter has highlighted the major survey developers and their datasets. In preparing for future use of national datasets, however, users need to be aware of a number of emerging trends that will impact their utility.

One of the first considerations is the ongoing availability of data. Because of a major budget shortfall in agency appropriations, many IPEDS data collections were sharply cut back in the 2000 reporting year. This cutback came at a time when NCES was moving these collections to the Web for the first time, after an exhaustive IPEDS redesign process. Therefore, users should expect that many data variables of interest may not be available for 2000. In restoring these data for 2001, NCES implemented the redesign recommendations of its NPEC Working Groups and task forces. Not all of the data cut in 2000 were fully restored. Users must check the continuity of data over time from 1999 through 2001, before expecting to find critical trend data.

Another issue impacting the availability of IPEDS data, however disseminated, involves changes in financial reporting mandated by the Financial Accounting Standards Board (FASB) which effect private not-for-private and private for-profit institutions, and the Government Accounting Standards Board (GASB), which effect public institutions. With the implementation of FASB in the late 1990s, and the imminent implementation of GASB, the comparison of public and private IPEDS Finance data is no longer possible. Also, the consistency of implementation within sectors is also in question. Therefore, some financial data are not yet available for this time period. Ongoing financial data may, or may not, be collected, depending upon the budget problem of 2000, the move to Web collection, the implementation of FASB/GASB, and the implementation of the IPEDS redesign.

Several new data collections are becoming available or are in the pilot phase. The IPEDS Employee by Assigned Position Survey was voluntary in 2001; however it is required in the 2002-03 cycle. A survey of Instructional Activity, allowing for measures of productivity, is being piloted as part of an

NCES Working Group. It is possible that these data could become part of IPEDS in the future. Some institutional characteristics data, such as average test scores, which have been part of the college admission guide's collection, are becoming part of IPEDS.

Posing a greater challenge to data comparability over time, the Office of Management and Budget (OMB) will require institutions to begin reporting about students and faculty using new race and ethnicity coding. The NSF GSS already incorporates this change. However, it is not yet completely clear that the final version of the coding will be what the GSS implemented. All trend and historical data about race and ethnicity will be lost once these new reporting requirements are fully implemented. During those years in which institutions struggle to adequately report the data until their systems are in place, the results may not be comparable.

Keeping Track of Changes

In order to keep track of these changes, dataset users should watch closely the NCES, NSF, and AIR Web sites. As part of its AIR/NCES/NSF grant program, titled "Improving Institutional Research in Postsecondary Educational Institutions," the Association for Institutional Research (AIR) promotes "opportunities for postsecondary education professionals and doctoral students to conduct research utilizing the national databases" through grants, institutes, and a post-masters certificate program. Additional information is available at: http://airweb.org/ and click on Professional Development.

One key resource for using the national datasets is the annual NCES/NSF Summer Database Institute, which trains approximately 40 fellows per year with a "combination of instruction on the content and uses of the NSF and NCES national data sets relevant to postsecondary education, and policy seminars focused on national postsecondary education issues." For those who cannot attend the Institute, a number of workshops and presentations about NCES, NSF, and other data collections are held at the annual AIR Forum and other regional and association conferences. For federal, SHEEO, and affiliated association staffers, the annual SHEEO/NCES Network has been in place since 1976, with an annual meeting and other important activities. One of the purposes of the SHEEO/NCES Network is to "make national and state data collections valuable and relevant to policymakers."

The Higher Education Data Policy Committee (HEDPC) of AIR works to promote communication regarding a number of data issues which impact users. The HEDPC Web site provides updates on the status of its projects. Additional information is available at the AIR Web site: http://airweb.org.

Another important feature of the AIR Web site is the Internet Resources for Institutional Research feature. Offered since 1995 and housing several thousand links in more than 80 categories, this Web site is the oldest and most complete source of online information about postsecondary education and is available at: http://airweb.org/ and click on IR Resources.

Finally, dataset uses should follow the work of the National Postsecondary Education Cooperative (NPEC). Congress authorized NCES, in 1994, to establish the Cooperative. Its mission is "to promote the quality, comparability, and utility of data for postsecondary decision-making at the national, state, and institutional levels." Additional information about NPEC is available at: http://nces.ed.gov/npec.

Summary

This chapter documents the many types of postsecondary education datasets, which are available to researchers, along with how they may be accessed and better understood. While the datasets and software tools are very complex, they are also very rich topically, with information to support many kinds of policy, research, and analytical studies. Much of the potential of these datasets has not been utilized.

Researchers are encouraged to make use of existing, national, sample and institutional datasets whenever appropriate, especially those from NCES and NSF. An enormous effort has been undertaken to transform the collection and dissemination of data from the printed survey form and magnetic tape of the early 1990's to the online data entry forms and analytical tools of today. With an exciting array of new data and software, researchers are encumbered with the responsibility to consider what these datasets have to offer.

References

Association for Institutional Research. (2002). NCES and NSF Postsecondary Datasets: Descriptive information about the purpose, respondents, key variables, target population and sample frame from popular NCES and NSF surveys. Tallahassee, FL: Association for Institutional Research.

Milam, J. H., Jr. (1999, Winter). *Using the National Datasets for Faculty Studies*. AIR Professional File, No. 70. Tallahassee, FL: Association for Institutional Research.

National Center for Education Statistics. (2002). Digest of Education Statistics, 2001. Washington, D.C.: U.S. Department of Education. http://nces.ed.gov/pubs2002/digest2001/index.asp.

Russell, A. B., and Winter, S. B. (2001). Compendium of National Data Sources on Higher Education. Fifth edition. SHEEO/NCES Communication Network. Denver, CO: State Higher Education Executive Officers.

End Notes

[1] The reader is referred to the author's AIR *Professional File* article titled "Using the National Datasets for Faculty Studies" (Milam, 1999), for a detailed treatment of how data may be used for this topic. Other examples of references using the datasets are included in ANSWERS, in SOAR, and on the NCES and NSF Web sites.

[2] Note that NSF's science and engineering disciplines includes social sciences.

Chapter 9
Records Management

Andrew L. Luna
Tara P. Pearson
State University of West Georgia.

Introduction

Institutional researchers have clearly accepted, if not embraced, the information age. Since its inception, the fundamental role of the IR office has been to provide accurate and timely information to aid in the planning and administration of higher education (Dressel, 1971; Suslow, 1971; Terenzini, 1993; Fincher, 1985). As technology has increased, so has the insatiable thirst of administrators, government officials, and the public at large for more facts and figures concerning higher education. Because of this increase in both the demand and supply of information, IR's role within colleges and universities has clearly gained popularity. In the process of generating the needed knowledge, the IR office has become somewhat of an information-production factory where raw material (data) are changed or processed into useable information about the institution (McLaughin & Howard, 2001).

In the past, all of this data collection and reporting was done by hand. Today, IR professionals use the computer to accomplish the majority of their work. No matter what the method used to acquire it, in the course of producing information, the IR office will receive, process, and generate many different types of records.

The purpose of this chapter is to inform the IR professional about the importance of records management and demonstrate how to create a comprehensive records management program. This chapter will also discuss the definitions, practices, and laws associated with records management as well as dispel many myths about records management, and the retention of important information.

Records Management

Information has both tangible and intangible value. It is important, therefore, that all information be properly managed, no matter if it originates from internal or external sources. Records management is a process in which the IR professional can identify what information has the highest value to the office and institution, where it should be kept, and how long it should be retained. The intent of an official records management program is to establish consistent record retention guidelines in compliance with state laws and requirements of external entities, such as governmental and accrediting agencies. A successful records management program can also provide legal protection, help the office or institution preserve the pertinent information, and facilitate finding the information the institution needs (Sanford, 2001).

150

A well-conceived and implemented records management program will present many financial benefits, as well. For example, an estimated 40 to 50 percent of the space used for records storage could be used for other purposes; the systematic disposal of records will prevent costly paper accumulation and, potentially, costly breaches of security to non-public records. Furthermore, other benefits to the IR office could include the protection from accidental or premature destruction of records, faster retrieval of reference material, and decrease purchases of excessive and expensive office filing equipment (Aschner, 1983).

What is the definition of a record, and how does the definition affect the IR office? According to many state laws, a general description of records are all documents, papers, letters, maps, books (except books in formally organized libraries), microfilm, magnetic tape, or other material, regardless of physical form or characteristic, that is made or received by an organization, that is useful in the operation of the organization (Georgia Department of Archives and History,1977; Haller, 1991) . Furthermore, according to these state laws, almost everything created or processed by an IR office is considered a record. Within the IR office, records can and should be divided into types, or series, of records. The following list identifies some of the record series usually found in a typical IR office:

- **Data Requests** – This series includes all reports, correspondence, and data files that relate to internal or external requests for information or data.

- **Surveys** – All external surveys (*i.e. U.S. News and World Report*, *Petersons*, *Wintergreen/Orchard House*, *Barrons*, etc.) and correspondence, working papers, and computer-generated reports associated with external surveys are included within this series.

- **Projects** – Any long-term assignment that takes longer to complete than a data request is grouped into this series. Examples could include salary equity studies, internal student satisfaction surveys, Fact Books, and annual reports. Included in this series are all correspondence, working papers, and computer generated reports associated with each project

- **Governing Agencies** – This series includes everything that is received from, or generated for, a board of regents, trustees, or post-secondary agency. Also included in this series are any working papers and computer generated reports associated with this series.

- **Institutional** – This series includes information originating in other departments, within the college or university, that is not associated with either data requests or projects. Examples could include other

151

departmental reports, policies, letters and correspondence not associated with data requests or projects, as well as general information about the institution.

- **Institutional Research** – This series includes all information generated by the IR office that is used internally to manage the office. Examples may include office policies, calendars, schedules, meeting minutes, as well as information from regional and national IR organizations.

- **Reference** – Any information that the office would like to keep for future referral is included in this series. This may include articles, conference material, and information on new procedures. This series can also include some records from other series that have reached their destruction date, but that the office would like to keep for future reference.

Again, this is only a partial list of the different types of record series that could be found in an IR office; types of records may differ depending upon the role, scope, and mission of the IR office within the college or university setting (Jones, 1989). It is important for the research to remember that a record series is a group of documents related in form or content and arranged under a single filing system or kept together as a unit. This grouping occurs because the series consists of the same forms, relates to the same subject, results from the same activity, or has certain similar physical characteristics (Haller, 1991).

From this abbreviated list, it is clear to see that an IR office collects, stores, manipulates, and generates many different types of records. The way in which IR professionals manage this voluminous material differs greatly from office to office and is predicated by the amount of training and knowledge the office is able to devote to records management. Unfortunately, within any office, including IR, myths and misconceptions exist regarding records and records management. Below are 10 of the most common:

1. **All records should be permanently stored**. In fact, few records should be kept permanently. Most records should be destroyed after their legally mandated retention period expires. This retention period varies by state and/or agency.

2. **As soon as files are destroyed, a need for them will arise**. If a record has been destroyed upon the expiration date of its legally mandated retention period, that record no longer exists. The office is no longer responsible for it, unless it fails to destroy the record. For example, the Internal Revenue Service requires individuals to keep tax records for only seven years. If the IRS requires an audit of one's personal records, the individual is only required to produce tax

records for this period of time. If, however, the individual has kept tax records for 20 years, and the IRS has knowledge of this, it may ask to review the full 20 years of records. Keeping records beyond their required retention period not only decreases office or personal space, it increases legal liability.

3. **That's not a record; it's a computer file**. Computer generated databases, reports, files, and e-mail are all considered records by state and federal laws. They should be treated the same as paper files and retained for the legally mandated amount of time required for that state for any non-computer record of similar type.

4. **A good spring-cleaning is all we need to do for records disposition**. In most states, it is illegal to randomly destroy records. For this reason, it is important to maintain retention schedules of your records and to document the life of a record from its beginning to its destruction or permanent storage.

5. **These are my records; it's nobody's business what I do with them**. All states have open records laws that apply to state-supported institutions. Depending on the state, records may include e-mail, calendars, letters, databases, reports, photographs, or tape recordings. State laws specify how long records should be kept, as well as which are open for public inspection. Furthermore, the Freedom of Information Act is a federal law that gives the public access to certain federal records generated by both public and private colleges and universities. Therefore, most records generated and maintained by an individual working in higher education are considered state or federal records; they are not owned by that individual.

6. **I don't need to worry about the files; the secretary or file clerk will take care of them**. The manner in which records are filed, retained, and destroyed is everybody's concern, especially the IR director. Not only is it important to be able to locate and retrieve files when they are needed, many outside organizations, such as special interest groups, government, and the media, are familiar with the state's records laws and can maximize these laws to their benefit. A records system that is well maintained, and understood by all within the IR office, will minimize any problems that may arise from records requests made by groups or individuals.

7. **Alphabetically, by subject, is the only way to file records**. While filing records by subject is a good way of tracking them, it is also important to manage records by date of creation and destruction (or permanent retention), as well as the type of series the record falls under in the state's retention policy.

8. **Office automation (computers) will reduce the amount of paper with which the IR office must deal with**. To the contrary, computers have

made the job of compiling reports much easier; therefore, more reports and records are being produced than ever before. While computers can make the job of filing and retrieval easier, paperwork will not likely be significantly reduced anytime in the near future. The IR office's electronic filing system should be maintained in the same manner as paper files, according to the state's retention policy.

9. **All of the IR offices' filing problems can be solved by putting old boxes of records in commercial storage or inside an unused room or building of the university**. It is not enough to store files; one must be able to find them. Furthermore, as storage space diminishes, the need to dispose of unneeded paper files is paramount to many administrators. While a state agency may not dispose of records until the specified retention period has expired, most IR offices will find that many of their currently stored records have long outlived their destruction dates.

10. **Anyone can file records.** A successful records management program insures that all staff are aware of filing, retrieval, and destruction of the office's records. Furthermore, an IR office that has created a records management process should systematically, and consistently, assess the effectiveness of its process and make changes where needed.

Vital Records and Disaster Plan

The most important objectives of a records management plan are the identification of the department's vital records and the creation of the department's disaster plan (Haller, 1991). Such processes can improve the protection of information and records that are vital to the IR department, improve overall management through better records administration, avoid unnecessary legal and fiscal problems, and help the IR department survive and recover from a disaster, resuming operations with minimum disruption and cost.

A vital record identification process is a critical element, and an integral part, of a comprehensive records management program. For a vital record identification process to be successful, only the most important records should be identified. State agencies define vital records as any record containing information essential for emergency operations during a disaster; the resumption and/or continuation of operations; the re-establishment of the legal, financial, and/or functional status of the organization; and the determination of the rights and obligations of individuals and corporate bodies with respect to the operation (Haller, 1991).

To identify vital records within the IR office, the director and staff should work together to understand the vital functions of the office. Then records should be identified which are essential to those functions (Aschner, 1983; Johnson & Kallaus, 1987). While it will be easy to identify some records as vital, greater strategic thinking will need to be exercised for the department's other records.

For example, the institution's official electronic data files for each term are easily identified as vital to the IR office; without these files, the office would no longer have point-in-time, historical file data from which to extract important information. On the other hand, the IR office may realize that the destruction of old external surveys and office correspondence will not significantly cripple operations.

Along with the vital record identification process is the creation of the disaster plan. Disasters can come from many different sources and vary in intensity. Disasters can include weather, fire, water damage, as well as the intentional destruction of records. A good disaster plan is simply a written set of procedures that prioritizes records, addresses disaster prevention, and outlines and guides disaster recovery efforts in case of an emergency (Aschner, 1983; Johnson & Kallaus,1987).

There are five essential questions an IR department must address in a good disaster plan:

1. **How are the vital records stored and/or duplicated?** Once the department has identified its vital records, it now needs to devise a plan to protect them. Whether they are computer generated files or paper files, the office should establish systematic and regular duplication and off-site storage of duplicate records. All vital records should be duplicated; the copies should be stored in another building or location away from the IR office (Aschner, 1983; Johnson & Kallaus, 1987).

2. **How important are the department's other files?** In this process, each record series that is not considered a vital record is examined and rated by level of importance. This rating system should be no more than four to five levels, ranging from very important to not important. A rating system will make it much easier for an office to concentrate its efforts on the most important files, leaving the least important ones, in the case of a major disaster (Aschner, 1983; Johnson & Kallaus 1987).

3. **How are records stored?** The storage of records is very important to their condition. If records are haphazardly stored in large, crushed boxes, they may not survive long-term retention. If the department's records are placed on the floor of a basement or stored below water pipes, where water damage is likely to occur, these conditions should be altered to minimize the effect of any potential disaster (Aschner, 1983; Johnson & Kallaus,1987).

4. **What is the institutional policy, if a disaster occurs?** The office should be familiar with the appropriate personnel to be notified, as well as the procedures to follow if a disaster occurs. Most institutional disaster plans are either on the Web or located within the public safety office (Aschner, 1983; Johnson & Kallaus, 1987).

5. **What is the department's plan for records protection/recovery?** Who in the office will be assigned to the tasks of cleaning, identification, and

temporary filing? How will damaged records be treated? For example, if records are under water, they can be placed in a bag with water, frozen in a commercial freezer, then taken to a recovery center to be freeze dried. A state's archives department is a good resource for information on records recovery (Aschner, 1983; Johnson & Kallaus, 1987).

Five Steps to Creating a Records Management Process

The records management system detailed in the following section is only an example; however, it does contain all of the essential elements in a successful records management plan. Initiating this plan requires only five steps, which can be easily implemented with very few forms and suitable records storage space and equipment. While the individual IR office may make variations to this plan, corresponding with its unique circumstances, it is important that each of the following five steps be followed to some extent.

1. **Inventory Phase** – This step is a potentially messy and dirty one. It requires that the IR office locate, identify, and record all IR records that are currently being filed, stored, boxed, or stashed away in a dark basement or closet. The inventory phase is the time to note how, and where, the records are being stored, as well as the approximate square footage of space the records are occupying (Aschner, 1983; Johnson, & Kallaus, 1987). Records will most likely be grouped in alphabetical order, by subject and year, rather than by record series. A well-labeled box or file folder will easily identify some of these records. Others will require almost detective-like thinking and creativity to identify. No matter how difficult or how dirty and dusty the work is, all records must be identified and recorded on an inventory form by the office. It is also important that, during this phase, no records are destroyed, regardless of how trivial or unimportant they may seem to be.

2. **Series Phase** – After all of the records have been identified, they must be placed in the appropriate record series by date. As was mentioned earlier, a record series is a group of documents, related in form or content, arranged under a single filing system or kept together as a unit. This grouping occurs because the records consist of the same forms, relate to the same subject, result from the same activity, or have certain similar physical characteristics. During this step, it may be helpful to set up file boxes for each record series and to place the appropriate records in them alphabetically, by subject and year (Aschner, 1983; Johnson, & Kallaus, 1987).

3. **Retention Phase** – Using the official retention schedule devised by either a state agency or the department's institution, determine the retention period for each series of records and create a series file indicating what is contained in the series, as well as the series retention period. If a series is not included in the retention plan, take the necessary steps to ensure that the series will be added to the schedule (Aschner, 1983; Johnson, & Kallaus, 1987).

4. **Storing/Labeling Phase** – After identifying and sorting all records according to the retention period, the records must then be stored and labeled so that everyone in the office understands the system. Ordinarily, the most current records will be kept in close proximity to the office; records from earlier periods may be kept in other places, such as a basement, institutional records storage center, or an off-site records center. It is also important to properly label records before storing them. A proper label should include the identification of the record series, name and year the record was created. A well-designed label should also contain the cut-off period (*i.e.* fiscal year, academic year); the transfer date, or date when the record will be moved from the office to the basement or off-site location; and the destruction date, if the record is not to be permanently stored (Aschner, 1983; Johnson, & Kallaus, 1987).

5. **Destruction Phase** – While some records should be permanently kept, based upon mandated retention guidelines, most records will need to be destroyed after their retention date expires. The destruction of records is a complex activity, requiring that specific procedures be followed. Individuals who have the authority to destroy records must also be identified. It is also important to document all steps leading up to, and including, the actual destruction of records. In general, most records slated for destruction should be shredded or burned, not placed into trash or recycling receptacles (Aschner, 1983; Johnson, & Kallaus, 1987).

Conclusion

It should be noted that, while there are many books and other resources available concerning records management, the state archives agency is probably the most useful and up-to-date source. Not only will it provide the department with comprehensive information on how to create a records management program, in most cases the agency has staff who are available to come to the department to inspect current records or advise on creating a new process.

Creating and maintaining a good records management program takes time, patience, and resources. It can also be a dirty and frustrating job. If done properly, however, a records management program can clearly become an added benefit to the IR office.

References

Aschner, K. (ed.) (1983). Taking control of your office records: A manager's guide. Boston, MA: G..K. Hall & Co.

Dressel, P. L and Associates. (1971). Institutional research in the university: A handbook. San Francisco, CA: Jossey-Bass.

Fincher, C. (1985). *The art and science of institutional research*. In M. Corcoran and M. W. Peterson (eds.). New Directions for Institutional Research: No. 46. Institutional research in transition. San Francisco, CA: Jossey-Bass. (pp. 17-37)

Georgia Department of Archives and History (1977). Files management. Publication 77-RM-1, Atlanta, GA: The Secretary of State.

Haller, S (1991). Managing records on limited resources: A guide for local governments. Washington D.C.: The National Association of Government Archives and Records Administrators.

Johnson, M. & Kallaus, N. (1987). Records management. Cincinnati, OH: South-Western Publishing Co.

Jones, L. (1989). *The institutional research report revisited*. In P. T. Ewell (ed.). New Directions for Institutional Research: No. 64. Enhancing information use in decision making. San Francisco, CA: Jossey-Bass.

McLaughlin, G. and Howard, R. (2001). *Theory, practice, and ethics of institutional research*. In R. Howard (Ed.) Institutional research: Decision support in higher education. Tallahassee, FL: Association for Institutional Research. (pp 163-194).

Sanford, T. (2001). *Records management for institutional research*. Paper presented at the Annual Conference of the Southern Association for Institutional Research. Panama Beach, FL.

Suslow, S. (1971). *Present reality of institutional research*. C. L. Stewart (Ed.), Presidential Address, 11th Annual Forum of the Association for Institutional Research. Tallahassee, FL: Association for Institutional Research.

Terenzini, P. T. (1993). *On the nature of institutional research and the knowledge and skills it requires*. The Journal of Research in Higher Education, 34(1), (pp. 1-10).

Conclusion

William E. Knight
Bowling Green State University

It was noted in the Introduction that previous *Primers*, the *Strategies for the Practice of Institutional Research* volume, and this update serve as just some of many professional development resources available to institutional researchers. The purpose of this concluding chapter is to highlight other resources. Additional information about many of the resources provided through the Association for Institutional Research (AIR) are available from the AIR Web site (http://www.airweb.org). Some of the many valuable features of the AIR Web site include the Internet Resources for Institutional Research page (which includes links to numerous organizations and resources), institutional research job listings, and information on conferences, publications, and other professional development opportunities.

Other volumes in AIR's *Resources in Institutional Research* (RIR) series that preceded this work include:

- *A Primer on Institutional Research* (1987; J.A. Muffo, G.W. McLaughlin)

- *The Functions of Institutional Research*, 2nd Edition (1990; J.L. Saupe)

- *Questionnaire Survey Research: What Works?* (1992; L.A. Suskie)

- *The Primer for Institutional Research* (1992; M.A. Whiteley, J.D. Porter, R.H. Fenske)

- *Reference Sources: An Annotated Bibliography for Institutional Research* (1993; W.F. Fendley, L.T. Seeloff)

- *Strategies for the Practice of Institutional Research: Concepts, Resources, and Applications* (1994; M.F. Middaugh, D.W. Trusheim, K.W. Bauer)

- *Case Study Applications of Statistics in Institutional Research* (1997; M.A. Coughlin, M. Pagano)

- *People, Processes, and Managing Data* (1998; G.W. McLaughlin, R.D. Howard, L.A. Balkan, E.W. Blythe)

- *Effective Reporting* (1999; T.H. Bers, J.A. Seybert)

- *Institutional Research: Decision Support in Higher Education* (2001, R. D. Howard)

It should be noted, however, that not all of these are currently in print.

AIR sponsors several other publications in addition to the RIR series. *Research in Higher Education* is an academically-oriented journal containing carefully selected papers by experts, stressing quantitative studies of college and university procedures. Six issues are published per year; special subscription rates are available for AIR members. Each annual issue of the *Higher Education Handbook of Theory and Research* provides an integrative literature review on 10-12 topics, contributing to the long-term development of a solid foundation of cumulative knowledge about higher education theory and research; special subscription rates are available for AIR members. Each single issue of the *New Directions for Institutional Research* series is devoted to a specific institutional research, planning, or policy topic, with chapters written by various experts. Issues are published quarterly; special subscription rates are available for AIR members. The *AIR Professional File*, published four times a year, is a presentation of papers that synthesize and interpret issues, operations, and research of interest in the field of institutional research; copies are provided, in print and on-line, to AIR members at no cost. The *Electronic AIR* is the AIR newsletter sent to subscribers every four weeks, via e-mail; contents include news items, comments about recent publications, job announcements, requests for help or suggestions from readers, announcements of professional meetings and conferences, abstracts of papers which authors are willing to share, persons relocating or promoted to new IR jobs or retiring, etc. The *AIR Currents* is a quarterly Web-based newsletter available to AIR members only. *AIR Currents* focuses on news about the association; state, regional, and special interest groups; and the field of institutional research. The *AIR Alerts* present the AIR membership with timely, substantive information on data policy issues, which may impact them in the future; the publication is made available on an at-need basis, in both print and Web format.

Perhaps AIR's most well known professional development opportunity for institutional researchers is its annual Forum. This national conference provides an abundance of opportunities for presentations, panels, demonstrations, workshops, and professional networking. Additional details about the Forum, including presentation materials submitted from past Forums, are available from AIR's web page. Selected presentation materials from AIR Forums are available through the ERIC Clearinghouse on Higher Education; *Research in Higher Education* also publishes an annual special Forum issue.

During the last few years, AIR has introduced a series of professional development institutes. These are multi-day workshops designed to focus upon specific topics and competencies essential to the profession. Faculty for the institutes include leading institutional research practitioners. Recent institutes have included Applied Statistics for Institutional Research, Planning, and Management; Foundations for the Practice of Institutional Research; Enrollment Management and Information Technology. Not all of the institutes are offered each year; consult the AIR Web page for additional information.

The AIR grant programs provide resources for institutional researchers and doctoral students to engage in targeted professional development opportunities. They are also designed to foster the use of federal databases as sources of information for institutional research. AIR, with support from the National Center for Education Statistics (NCES) and the National Science Foundation (NSF), has developed a program titled: *Improving Institutional Research in Postsecondary Educational Institutions*. The program has four major components: (a) dissertation research grants for doctoral students including the Charles I. Brown Fellowship award for the outstanding dissertation proposal, (b) research grants for practitioners and faculty, (c) a senior fellowship program, and (d) a Summer Data Policy Institute in the Washington, D.C. area, dedicated to the study of the national databases of NSF and NCES. For additional information, consult AIR's Web site (http://www.airweb.org).

Numerous AIR state, provincial, regional and international affiliates and special interest groups exist to advance the professional development needs of members and the aims of the association within designated geographic areas or topical interests.

AIR has established several member committees that are designed to foster the effectiveness and ongoing professional development of institutional researchers. The Higher Education Data Policy Committee serves as a forum for identification and discussion of timely and relevant data policy issues affecting institutional researchers; the committee also serves as a vehicle for advising various external organizations. The Professional Development Services Committee provides leadership for meeting the professional development needs of members.

A number of organizations, in addition to AIR, provide information, resources, and professional development opportunities that are beneficial to institutional researchers. Among these organizations are the Society for College and University Planning (http://www.scup.org), the National Association of College and University Business Officers (http://www.nacubo.org), the American Association for Higher Education (http://www.aahe.org), the American Council on Education (http://www.acenet.edu), the Association for the Study of Higher Education (http://www.ashe.missouri.edu), the National Center for Educational Statistics (http://nces.ed.gov), the American College Testing Program (http://www.act.org), Educational Testing Service (http://www.ets.org), John Minter Associates (http://www.jma-inc.net), the National Center for Higher Education Management Systems (http://www.nchems.org), the Southern Regional Education Board (http://www.sreb.org/), and the Western Interstate Consortium for Higher Education (http://www.wiche.edu/home.htm).

Some of the non-AIR-sponsored publications that may prove valuable to institutional researchers include *Campus Trends*, *Change*, the *Chronicle of Higher Education*, *Higher Education and National Affairs*, the *Journal of Higher Education*, *On the Horizon*, and *Review of Higher Education*.

This Conclusion was designed to provide a concise listing of professional development opportunities and resources available to institutional researchers. Despite all best efforts, it is likely incomplete and in need of updates soon after publication. I offer my apologies for valuable sources that may have been left out and urge readers to check the AIR Web site, and other sources, for updates.